WHY READ AND STUDY THE BOOKS OF PROVERBS, ECCLESIASTES, AND JAMES?

If you think that the real test of religion is how it works out in everyday life, you're not alone. Several books in the Bible look primarily at how believing in God can help a person live the best possible life right here and now, on this earth.

These books—Proverbs, Ecclesiastes, and James*—explain how to draw on your faith to develop a style of practical living that's honest, generous, and fair. They do this by sharing insights preserved in short, memorable sayings passed down from generation to generation. Some of these sayings make provocative observations that invite us to reflect on life: "Those who love money never have enough; those who love wealth are never satisfied with their income." Other sayings use illustrations drawn from the natural world: "Can both fresh water and salt water flow from the same spring?" And many make a striking impression through the vivid pictures they create: "Like one who grabs a stray dog by the ears is one who rushes into a quarrel not their own."

---

* Maybe you're surprised that James is included in this study guide with two books from the First Testament. James is often grouped with the letters in the New Testament, but it actually has much more in common with Proverbs and Ecclesiastes than it does with those letters. The book of James is concerned with practical living as an expression of genuine faith, and it communicates through short statements and vivid illustrations just like Proverbs and Ecclesiastes. You'll find out more about this when you experience the book of James as a whole in session 21.

For followers of Jesus, life in the age to come is going to be great—but how about some life before death? If you want to see the impact that believing in God can have on your daily life right now, get together with some friends and explore the timeless wisdom that these books have to share.

UNDERSTANDING THE
BOOKS OF THE BIBLE

PROVERBS, ECCLESIASTES, and JAMES

Also available in the
UNDERSTANDING THE BOOKS OF THE BIBLE series:

John
Genesis
Biblical Apocalypses: Daniel/Revelation
Joshua/Judges/Ruth—March 2011
Thessalonians/Corinthians/Galatians/Romans—March 2011

Future releases:

Exodus/Leviticus/Numbers
New Covenants: Deuteronomy/Hebrews
Samuel–Kings

Amos/Hosea/Micah/Isaiah
Zephaniah/Nahum/Habakkuk
Jeremiah/Obadiah/Ezekiel
Haggai/Zechariah/Jonah/Joel/Malachi

Psalms Books 1–3
Psalms Books 4–5/Song of Songs/Lamentations
Job
Chronicles/Ezra/Nehemiah/Esther

Matthew
Mark
Luke–Acts

Colossians/Ephesians/Philemon/Philippians/Timothy/Titus
Peter/Jude/John

UNDERSTANDING THE BOOKS OF THE BIBLE

PROVERBS, ECCLESIASTES, and JAMES

Christopher R. Smith

Transforming lives through God's Word

Transforming lives through God's Word

Biblica provides God's Word to people through translation, publishing and Bible engagement in Africa, Asia Pacific, Europe, Latin American, Middle East, and North America. Through its worldwide reach, Biblica engages people with God's Word so that their lives are transformed through a relationship with Jesus Christ.

Biblica Publishing
We welcome your questions and comments.

1820 Jet Stream Drive, Colorado Springs, CO 80921 USA
www.Biblica.com

UNDERSTANDING THE BOOKS OF THE BIBLE: Proverbs/Ecclesiastes/James
ISBN-13: 978-1-60657-056-2

A catalog record for this book is available through the Library of Congress.

Printed in the United States of America

CONTENTS

FOR LEADERS
How These Study Guides Are Different   1

PROVERBS

SESSION 1
The Wise and Foolish Ways of Life   13

SESSION 2
Everything You Do Flows from Your "Heart"   16

SESSION 3
The "Heart" Expressed by How We Use Money and How We Speak   21

SESSION 4
The "Heart" Expressed in Relationships and Reputation   26

SESSION 5
What Brings the Content of the Heart out into Key Areas of Life   30

SESSION 6
Receiving and Giving Correction   34

SESSION 7
Character Qualities: The Fear of the LORD   38

SESSION 8
Character Qualities: Humility   42

SESSION 9
Character Qualities: Self-control   45

SESSION 10
Character Qualities: Diligence (Hard Work)   49

SESSION 11
Character Qualities: Dependability   53

SESSION 12
Character Qualities: Caution (Prudence)   57

SESSION 13
Character Qualities: Justice   61

SESSION 14
Warnings Against Drunkenness and Sexual Immorality   66

SESSION 15
Warnings Against Gangs and Putting Up Security   70

ECCLESIASTES

SESSION 16
Experiencing the Book of Ecclesiastes as a Whole   77

SESSION 17
Insights from Experience   83

SESSION 18
Insights from Observation   89

SESSION 19
The Practical Response to These Insights   94

SESSION 20
Concluding Thoughts and Observations: "Remember Your Creator"   98

JAMES

SESSION 21
Experiencing the Book of James as a Whole   107

SESSION 22
The Value of Trials   111

SESSION 23
The Rich and the Poor from God's Perspective   116

SESSION 24
Keeping a Tight Rein on the Tongue   120

SESSION 25
The Life that Flows from a New Heart   124

HOW THESE STUDY GUIDES
ARE DIFFERENT

Did you know you could read and study the Bible without using any chapters or verses? The books of the Bible are real "books." They're meant to be experienced the same way other books are: as exciting, interesting works that keep you turning pages right to the end and then make you want to go back and savor each part. The UNDERSTANDING THE BOOKS OF THE BIBLE series of study guides will help you do that with the Bible.

While you can use these guides with any version or translation, they're especially designed to be used with *The Books of The Bible,* an edition of the Scriptures from Biblica that takes out the chapter and verse numbers and presents the biblical books in their natural form. Here's what people are saying about reading the Bible this way:

I love it. I find myself understanding Scripture in a new way, with a fresh lens, and I feel spiritually refreshed as a result. I learn much more through stories being told, and with this new format, I feel the truth of the story come alive for me.

Reading Scripture this way flows beautifully. I don't miss the chapter and verse numbers. I like them gone. They got in the way.

I've been a reader of the Bible all of my life. But after reading just a few pages without chapters and verses, I was amazed at what I'd been missing all these years.

For more information about *The Books of The Bible* or to obtain a low-cost copy, visit http://www.thebooksofthebible.info. Premium editions of this Bible will be available in Spring 2011 from Zondervan at your favorite Christian retailer.

For people who are used to chapters and verses, reading and studying the Bible without them may take a little getting used to. It's like when you get a new cell phone or upgrade the operating system on your computer. You have to unlearn some old ways of doing things and learn some new ways. But it's not too long until you catch on to how the new system works and you find you can do a lot of things you couldn't do before.

Here are some of the ways you and your group will have a better experience of the Scriptures by using these study guides.

YOU'LL FOLLOW THE NATURAL FLOW OF BIBLICAL BOOKS

This guide will take you through the books of Proverbs, Ecclesiastes, and James following their natural flow. (The way these first two books unfold is illustrated in the outlines on pages 11 and 82.) You won't go chapter-by-chapter through these books, because chapter divisions in the Bible often come at the wrong places and break up the flow. Did you know that the chapter divisions used in most modern Bibles were added more than a thousand years after the biblical books were written? And that the verse numbers were added more than three centuries after that? If you grew up with the chapter-and-verse system, it may feel like part of the inspired Word of God. But it's not. Those little numbers aren't holy, and when you read and study Proverbs, Ecclesiastes, and James without them, you'll hear their message more clearly than ever before.

To help you get a feel for where you are in each book's natural flow, the readings in Proverbs and the sessions in Ecclesiastes will be headed by a visual cue, like this:

Book of Proverbs > Sayings of Agur

YOU'LL UNDERSTAND WHOLE BOOKS

Imagine going to a friend's house to watch a movie you've never seen before. After only a couple of scenes, your friend stops the film and says, "So, tell me what you think of it so far." When you give your best shot at a reply, based on the little you've seen, your friend says, "You know, there's a scene in another movie that always makes me think of this one." He switches to a different movie and before you know it, you're watching a scene from the middle of another film.

Who would ever try to watch a movie this way? Yet many study guides take this approach to the Bible. They have you read a few paragraphs from one book, then jump to a passage in another book. The UNDERSTANDING THE BOOKS OF THE BIBLE series doesn't do that. Instead, these study guides focus on understanding the message and meaning of one book at a time. Your group will read through the entire books of Proverbs, Ecclesiastes, and James, not just selected chapters or verses.

Two of the sessions (session 16 and session 21) are overviews that will let you experience the books of Ecclesiastes and James as a whole, to prepare you for considering their individual sections. Reading through an entire book at once will be like viewing a whole movie before zooming in on one scene. Groups that read books of the Bible aloud together have a great experience doing this. (If you've never done it before, give it a try—you'll be surprised at how well it flows and how fast the time passes.) For these overview sessions, the discussion will be briefer and designed to allow people to share their overall impressions.

The book of Proverbs has to be approached a bit differently. It's a collection of originally independent sayings that are each meant to strike the hearer with freshness and immediacy. Reading through the entire collection at once, without allowing for reflection and impact, dulls the edge of these sayings. So in the case of this book, it's better to work up from the parts to the whole. You'll read it a little at a time each week, noting the proverbs that speak immediately to your life, and as you go along you'll also explore and discuss the overall message of the book. But Proverbs actually begins with a series of longer speeches, words of challenge and encouragement spoken by parents to their children, that set the tone for the whole book and introduce its themes. It's helpful to read and discuss these all at once, and that's what you'll do in session 1.

Note to group leaders: Each member should bring a Bible and a pencil, pen, highlighter, notebook, laptop, or some other means of noting meaningful individual sayings each week as you read and discuss the book of Proverbs. You may want to have some extras available in case they're needed.

YOU'LL DECIDE FOR YOURSELVES WHAT TO DISCUSS

In each session of this study guide there are many options for discussion. While each session could be completed by a group in about an hour and a half, any one of the questions could lead to an involved conversation. There's no need to cut the conversation short to try to "get through it all." As a group leader, you can read through all the questions ahead of time and decide which one(s) to begin with, and what order to take them up in. If you do get into an involved discussion of one question, you can leave out some of the others, or you can extend the study over more than one meeting if you do want to cover all of them.

TOGETHER, YOU'LL TELL THE STORY

Each session gives creative suggestions for reading the passage you'll be discussing. If you're using *The Books of The Bible*, you'll find that the natural sections it marks off by white space match up with the sections of the reading. If you're using another edition of the Bible, you'll be able to identify these sections easily because they'll be indicated in this guide by their opening lines, or by some other means that makes them obvious.

EVERYBODY WILL PARTICIPATE

There's plenty of opportunity for everyone in the group to participate. Everyone can take turns reading the sayings from Proverbs, Ecclesiastes, and James that you'll be considering. Group members can also read the session introduction aloud or the discussion questions. As a leader, you can easily involve quiet people by giving them these opportunities. And everyone will feel that they can speak up and answer the questions, because they're not looking for "right answers." Instead, they invite the group to work together to understand the Bible.

YOU'LL ALL SHARE DEEPLY

The discussion questions will invite you to share deeply about your ideas and experiences. The answers to these questions can't be found just by "looking them up." They require reflection on the meaning of each saying, in the wider context of the book it belongs to, in light of your personal experience. These aren't the kinds of abstract, academic questions that make the discussion feel like a test. Instead, they'll connect the Bible passage to your life in practical, personal, relational ways.

To create a climate of trust where this kind of deep sharing is encouraged, here are a couple of ground rules that your group should agree to at its first meeting:

Confidentiality. Group members agree to keep what is shared in the group strictly confidential. "What's said in the group stays in the group."

Respect. Group members will treat other members with respect at all times, even when disagreeing over ideas.

HOW TO LEAD GROUP STUDIES USING THIS GUIDE

Each session has three basic parts:

Introduction to the Study

Have a member of your group read the introduction to the session out loud to everyone. Then give group members the chance to ask questions about the introduction and offer their own thoughts and examples.

Reading from Proverbs, Ecclesiastes, and James

Read the selection out loud together. (The study guide will offer suggestions for various ways you can do this for each session. For the book of James, reading and discussion are combined.)

Discussion Questions

Most questions are introduced with some observations. These may give some background to the history and culture of the ancient world, or explain where you are in the flow of the book. After these observations there are suggested discussion questions. Many of them have multiple parts that are really just different ways of getting at an issue.

You don't have to discuss the questions in the order they appear in the study guide. You can choose to spend your time exploring just one or two questions and not do the others. Or you can have a shorter discussion of each question so that you do cover all of them. As the group leader, before the meeting you should read the questions and the observations that introduce them, and decide which ones you want to emphasize.

When you get to a given question, have someone read aloud the observations and the question. As you answer the question, interact with the observations (you can agree or disagree with them) in light of your reading from the Bible. Use only part of the question to get at the issue from one angle, or use all of the parts, as you choose.

TIPS FOR HOME GROUPS, SUNDAY SCHOOL CLASSES, COMMUNITY BIBLE EXPERIENCES, AND INDIVIDUAL USE

If you're using this guide in a *home group*, you may want to begin each meeting (or at least some meetings) by having dinner together. You may also want to have a time of singing and prayer before or after the study.

If you're using this guide in a *Sunday school class*, you may want to have a time of singing and prayer before or after the study.

This study guide can also be used in connection with a *community Bible experience* of the books of Proverbs, Ecclesiastes, and James. If you're using it in this way:

- Encourage people to read each session's Scripture passage by themselves early in the week (except for sessions 1, 16, and 21, when the whole church will gather to hear the opening speeches in Proverbs and the books of Ecclesiastes and James read out loud).
- Do each session in midweek small groups.
- Invite people to write/create some response to each small-group session that could be shared in worship that weekend. These might involve poetry, journal or blog entries, artwork, dramas, videos, and so on.
- During the weekend worship services, let people share these responses, and have preaching on the topic of the session that was studied that week. Speakers can gather up comments they've heard from people and draw on their own reflections to sum up the church's experience of that session.

This guide can also be used for *individual study*. You can write out your responses to the questions in a notebook or journal. (However, we really encourage reading and studying the Bible in community!)

Note: Anytime you see *italicized* words in Scripture quotations in this book, the italics have been added for emphasis.

PROVERBS

CHARACTER QUALITIES: HUMILITY

INTRODUCTION

In the next several sessions, we'll look at specific character qualities that the fear of the LORD, informed by wisdom and knowledge, and empowered by the Holy Spirit, builds into our lives. We'll begin in this session with an essential quality that, unknown to the less wise, is a person will be wise or foolish, wicked or righteous. Humility determines how willing a person is to receive correction. This is the quality of humility—it is the opposite of pride.

READING

Take turns reading the next several proverbs in the miniature collection of Solomon's proverbs, beginning with "The poor are shunned by all their relatives—how much more do their friends avoid them!" and ending with "The human spirit is the lamp of the LORD that sheds light on one's inmost being."

COLLECTIONS OF SAYINGS IN
THE BOOK OF PROVERBS

Opening Speeches (12)
The first speech is a prologue to the book

Proverbs of Solomon (375)
The value of the Hebrew letters in Solomon's name is 375

"Sayings of the Wise" (30)

More "Sayings of the Wise" (5)

Proverbs of Solomon (130)
"compiled by the men of Hezekiah"
The value of the Hebrew letters in Hezekiah's name is 130

The Sayings of Agur

The Sayings of King Lemuel

The poem about a "wife of noble character" may be by another wise person

THE WISE AND FOOLISH WAYS OF LIFE

INTRODUCTION

The book of Proverbs is made up of several collections of practical sayings, passed down from generation to generation, that represent the distilled wisdom of experience. (See the outline on page 11.) Solomon, the third king of Israel, was renowned for his wisdom, and he was an avid collector and creator of proverbs. This book preserves over five hundred of his proverbs, as well as the sayings of other wise people of the ancient world.

Before the collections of sayings begin, the book of Proverbs presents a series of speeches that praise the practical benefits a person can receive by pursuing the wisdom that's embodied in these sayings. These speeches make up the first third of the book and set the tone for Proverbs as a whole by introducing its overall themes.

Above all, the speeches establish a fundamental contrast between being "wise" and being "foolish." These terms don't refer to how intelligent or educated a person is. This is moral and spiritual language. The "wise" person always takes God into account when choosing a course of action. This way of proceeding is spoken of as the "fear of the LORD."* By contrast, "fools" live without regard to God. They don't necessarily deny that God exists; they just live as if God didn't matter, and as if no one else had anything to teach them. These speeches describe in vivid detail how differently the life of a "fool" turns out from the life of a person who is "wise."

This session will get you into the book of Proverbs by taking you through the opening speeches that introduce its message and themes. (We'll have occasion to revisit these speeches often as we trace the major themes of the book in the following sessions.)

READING

Have the people in your group take turns reading the speeches at the beginning of the Proverbs. This should take about 45 minutes. Listen for the major themes these speeches develop, particularly the contrast between the "wise" and the "fool" and how their lives turn out differently.

Whenever something strikes you with freshness and immediacy, and you hear it speaking to your life today, mark it in some way. You might want to highlight or underline it in your Bible, or put a star next to it in the margin, or record it in a notebook or on a laptop computer. As you continue to note meaningful sayings week by week, you'll build a personal collection of proverbs that you can refer to as you apply the larger themes of the book to your own life.

In *The Books of The Bible*, the opening speeches in the book of Proverbs are on pages 1123–37. There are a couple of blank lines between each speech.

If you're using another edition of the Bible, you can recognize them from their opening lines:

- "The proverbs of Solomon son of David" (This speech

---

* "LORD" written in large and small capital letters is a translation of the divine name "Yahweh."

announces the book's purpose.)
- "Listen, my son, to your father's instruction . . ."
- "Out in the open wisdom calls aloud . . ."
- "My son, if you accept my words . . ."
- "My son, do not forget my teaching . . ."
- "Listen, my sons, to a father's instruction . . ." (ending, "keep your foot from evil")
- "My son, pay attention to my wisdom . . ."
- "My son, if you have put up security for your neighbor . . ."
- "My son, keep your father's command . . ."
- "My son, keep my words and store up my commands . . ."
- "Does not wisdom call out? . . ."
- "Wisdom has built her house . . ." (ending just before the heading "The proverbs of Solomon")

DISCUSSION

◑ What things struck you most as you listened to the opening speeches in the book of Proverbs? If you'd like, share one or two of the statements you highlighted for yourself, and explain why they were meaningful for you.

◑ What's the main advice that's given in these speeches? How would you express it in your own words?

◑ Proverbs was written a long time ago, but its sayings are meant to be timeless. What are some present-day examples of the kinds of things these speeches are talking about?

EVERYTHING YOU DO FLOWS FROM YOUR "HEART"

INTRODUCTION

As you read through the book of Proverbs session by session, storing up its wisdom by recording and reflecting on individual statements that strike you, you'll also be discussing its major themes and overall message.

It won't be possible to synchronize the reading and discussion exactly for each session. The sayings in the book of Proverbs aren't organized by topic; instead, within each of the collections in the book, observations on a variety of topics are all mixed together, so that each one can strike the hearer with fresh force. People who work through Proverbs *collection by collection*, talking about whatever sayings they find most interesting, will certainly have a lively and freewheeling discussion every time. But they won't necessarily appreciate the foundational message of the book and recognize how this finds expression through its individual sayings.

Another approach would be to consider the proverbs in *topical groups*. The book provides practical advice on a variety of subjects: work, money, friendship, marriage, sex, parenting, food, drink, health, speech, anger, crime, death, and so forth. However, there's a danger in approaching the book this way. It's not providing practical advice that just anyone can follow to be happy and successful in life. At its deepest level, the book of Proverbs is trying to show us how to *become the kind of people* who can live in the wise way it describes.

This is the fundamental theme of the book, and we'll begin exploring it in this session. In the sessions that follow we'll continue this *thematic approach*, drawing on proverbs from all over the book. Each time you'll read more of Proverbs and continue to mark and collect the sayings that strike you most. You'll find that many of them will relate to the discussion topics that are raised. And by the time you reach the end of the book in session 15, you should be able to see its full thematic message expressed in the sayings you've found most meaningful to your life right now.

In this guide, it will only be possible to cite and discuss a small percentage of the proverbs in the book. These represent many others that shed further light on the same areas of life, from complementary perspectives. Any one proverb could easily provide the basis of an entire evening's discussion. But since a group that meets weekly would need well over a decade to go through the book that way, these representative proverbs are offered to introduce you to the book and hopefully to generate a life-long interest in its collection of provocative and empowering sayings.

READING

After the opening speeches, the book of Proverbs presents several collections of short sayings that express the wisdom of experience in a concise and memorable way. The first collection is of 375 of Solomon's proverbs. In Hebrew, letters were also used as numbers, and 375 is the total value of the letters in Solomon's name. This is therefore a "signature collection" of some of his most insightful and telling observations about life.

Have the members of your group take turns reading the first 25 proverbs in this collection, ending with "When the storm has swept by, the wicked are gone, but the righteous stand firm forever." After each proverb, pause briefly so that people can absorb its meaning and highlight it for themselves if they wish. If anyone doesn't understand one of the proverbs, they should say so, and the group as a whole can help explain it. (You'll read a larger number of proverbs in later sessions; this session is designed to get you started on reading, reflecting, and recording.)

You might want to put a small mark, paper clip, or sticky note in your Bible at the place where you stopped reading, so that you can easily find your starting place for the next session. This may be helpful throughout your study of Solomon's proverbs, because there are so many of them, with no natural breaks. (The traditional chapter numbers are artificial divisions, so to give you a sense of where the real breaks in the book are, we're ignoring chapter divisions and just reading collection by collection.)

At the end of the reading, let people mention one or two proverbs that particularly struck them and explain how they spoke to their lives.

DISCUSSION

The foundational insight of the book of Proverbs is that each person has a core of being, known as the "heart." Everything a person thinks, says, and does flows out of this core. The sixth opening speech warns, "Above all else, guard your heart, for everything you do flows from it." Towards the end of the book, in a later collection of Solomon's proverbs, we're told, "As water reflects the face, so one's life reflects the heart." Who we truly are, deep inside, will inevitably come out in our words and actions.

The problem is, our "heart" or core-of-being is so deep within us that it's difficult to understand. It's hard for someone else to know: "Each heart knows its own bitterness, and no one else can share its joy." Our own heart is even hard for us to know: "People may think all their ways are right, but the LORD weighs the heart." This is why we may often feel that we don't really know who we are, and why we find ourselves wondering, "Why did I do that? How could I have said that?"

But there's hope. God, who knows the deepest secrets of the universe, can see into our hearts: "Death and destruction lie open before the

Lord—how much more do human hearts!" As a person lives in closer and closer relationship with God, and as they pray for understanding, God can show them what's in their heart. And the more godly wisdom someone acquires, the more clearly they can see into the depths of people's hearts—including their own: "The purposes of the human heart are deep waters, but those who have insight draw them out."

(If this topic is of particular interest to you, keep an eye out for the many other proverbs in the book that talk about the "heart.")

⟳ How well would you say you know yourself? Where would you place yourself on a scale of 1 to 10, with 10 being deep, consistent, accurate self-knowledge, and 1 being the place where you often say, "I don't think I really know who I am"?

⟳ If you feel comfortable doing so, share an experience, if you've had one recently, where you did or said something and then immediately wondered why you had. Were you eventually able to figure out what led you to speak or act as you did?

⟳ Who do you know who's best able to help you understand what's really going on inside you? What personal qualities make them good at this?

⟳ Conclude this session by praying together that God would reveal each of your own hearts to you. Begin by reading this prayer from Psalm 139 together:
Search me, God, and know my heart;
test me and know my anxious thoughts.
See if there is any offensive way in me,
and lead me in the way everlasting.

Then let anyone who wishes pray out loud. End by saying this ancient prayer together:

Most High, glorious God, enlighten the darkness of my heart, and give me right faith, certain hope, and perfect charity, wisdom and understanding, Lord, that I may carry out your holy and true command. Amen.

THE "HEART" EXPRESSED BY HOW WE USE MONEY AND HOW WE SPEAK

INTRODUCTION

In this session you'll read more of the "signature collection" of Solomon's proverbs, and you'll continue discussing Proverbs' theme of the "heart" as the core of being.

Most of the sayings in this collection are made up of two lines. These lines work together in one of three basic ways:

1. The second line may draw a contrast with the first: "Wise children bring joy to their father, but foolish children bring grief to their mother."

2. The second line may repeat the meaning of the first line, to reinforce it: "Hopes placed in mortals die with them; all the promise of their power comes to nothing." (Similarly, the two lines may be used to create a comparison: "As vinegar to the teeth and smoke to the eyes, so are sluggards to those who send them.")

3. The second line may add something to what the first line says: "The blessing of the LORD brings wealth, without painful toil for it."

As you listen to these proverbs, notice how the two lines are working together in one of these ways.

READING

Take turns reading the next 50 proverbs in this collection, beginning with "As vinegar to the teeth and smoke to the eyes, so are sluggards to those who send them," and ending with "The wicked desire the plunder of evildoers, but the root of the righteous flourishes." Remember to pause briefly after each proverb to let the meaning sink in and to work as a group to understand any sayings that aren't clear. People should continue to note the sayings that particularly strike them. After the reading, give people a chance to talk about one or two proverbs they found especially meaningful for their own lives.

DISCUSSION

1 We saw in the last session that every person has a core-of-being, or "heart," that's difficult to know because it lies so deep within them. However, because everything anyone says or does flows from their heart, its character and quality can be seen in certain personal spheres that express what's in the heart.

The first of these spheres is money. Money is a prime area where the heart overflows because it gives us the capability to fulfill our desires. So long as we can afford it, we can pretty much get anything we want.

But money also reveals what's in a person's heart another way. Not how much money they have, but *what kind* of money they have, shows how they've been living their life. Those who are wise, who live in the fear of the LORD, will accumulate "good money." It will last a long time and bring joy and satisfaction with it. Those who live without regard to God will acquire "bad money." Even if they make lots of it, it will come with trouble, and soon disappear. So Proverbs often cautions that we shouldn't pursue money as an end in itself. But if we pursue wisdom, a steadily increasing supply of "good money" will ordinarily be a by-product.

⊃ Do you know anyone who suddenly came into a lot of money (such as by winning the lottery, receiving an inheritance, or getting an insurance settlement), and was able to buy pretty much anything they wanted? What did they do with this money? How long did it last? What did their use of the money say about what was in their hearts?

⊃ Read each of the following proverbs aloud and decide whether it's describing "good money" or "bad money," or drawing a contrast between the two:

- "A fortune made by a lying tongue is a fleeting vapor and a deadly snare."
- "The blessing of the LORD brings wealth, without painful toil for it." (Or, "no trouble comes with it.")
- "Dishonest money dwindles away, but whoever gathers money little by little makes it grow."
- "Whoever increases wealth by taking interest or profit from the poor amasses it for another, who will be kind to the poor."
- "Good people leave an inheritance for their children's children, but a sinner's wealth is stored up for the righteous."
- "The house of the righteous contains great treasure, but the income of the wicked brings ruin."

Once you've discussed these proverbs, have each person in the group complete these sentences and share their answers:

"Good money is . . ."

"Bad money is . . ."

(If you've noted other proverbs on this same topic, draw on them to help fill out the portrait of the two kinds of money.)

⊃ Do you know a person or family that has "bad money"? Why would you describe their money this way? Do you know a person or family that has "good money"? What makes it good?

◑ If someone could see all of your expenses for the past year, how would they describe your priorities in life?

2 What a person says, particularly when they're free to say whatever they want, is a second area of life where their heart is directly expressed. To put it simply, what's in your heart will come out of your mouth. "The hearts of the wise make their mouths prudent, and their lips promote instruction." "Stay away from the foolish, for you will not find knowledge on their lips."

In this area as well, what matters is quality, not quantity. Just because a person is a "real talker," never at a loss for words, this doesn't make them wise. Indeed, the more a person talks, the more they may be trying to hide, excuse, or rationalize. "Sin is not ended by multiplying words, but the prudent hold their tongues." (Or, to paraphrase, "whenever there are many words, something wrong is probably going on.") Proverbs encourages us to speak valuable words, in prudent quantities, that will be a blessing to others, not a constant stream of worthless or deceptive words. "The tongue of the righteous is choice silver, but the heart of the wicked is of little value." "The mouth of the righteous is a fountain of life, but the mouth of the wicked conceals violence."

◑ Often we excuse something we've said by insisting, "Oh, I didn't really mean that." If words inevitably express what's in the heart, can a person ever really say something they don't mean?

◑ Think of a person who's been helpful and influential in your life. Are there particular sayings of theirs that you remember and repeat, treasuring them like "choice silver"? Share one or more of these sayings with the group.

(If the topics of money and speech are of particular interest to you, keep an eye out for the many other proverbs that talk about them.)

THE "HEART" EXPRESSED IN RELATIONSHIPS AND REPUTATION

Book of Proverbs > Solomon's Proverbs, continued

INTRODUCTION

In this session you'll continue reading Solomon's proverbs, and you'll discuss two more areas of life where the "heart," the core of being, finds direct expression.

As you read these proverbs, recognize that they aren't *commandments*. They're not orders to follow. Many of them would be difficult to put into practice as commandments, for example, the pair that says "Do not answer fools according to their folly, or you yourself will be just like them" and "Answer fools according to their folly, or they will be wise in their own eyes." (If these are orders, they're contradictory!)

These proverbs also aren't *promises*. Some of them would be very encouraging to take that way, such as, "Do you see those who are skilled in their work? They will serve before kings, they will not serve before officials of low rank." ("I promise that if you do good work, you'll get an influential position.") But others would be discouraging and even disturbing if we thought they were promises, such as, "The poor are shunned by all their relatives—how much more do their friends avoid them!" ("I promise that everyone will abandon you if you ever fall on hard times"?)

"The wicked accept bribes in secret to pervert the course of justice." ("I promise you'll be able to bribe your way out of legal trouble"?)

No, these proverbs are essentially *observations*, drawing on the wisdom of experience, about how life tends to work. As we've been seeing, what's in a person's heart will ultimately determine what happens throughout their life. So these proverbs aren't quick and easy ways for just anyone to find success. For those who live without regard to God, these sayings are just words. "Like the useless legs of one who is lame is a proverb in the mouth of a fool." The path of wisdom only opens up before people whose hearts are being reshaped as they live in the "fear of the LORD."

READING

Take turns reading the next 50 proverbs in this collection, beginning with "Evildoers are trapped by their sinful talk, and so the innocent escape trouble," and ending with "Fools mock at making amends for sin, but goodwill is found among the upright."

Continue to mark the proverbs that speak particularly to you, and share one or two of them after the reading.

DISCUSSION

1 Our relationships are a third area of life where what's in our heart gets expressed. It's revealed, first of all, in *what kind* of friends we have. Like attracts like. The more our hearts have been shaped by the "fear of the LORD," the more we will make friends with wise, godly people. The more we live without regard for God, the more we will make friends who don't care about God, and who won't care about us, either. "The righteous choose their friends carefully, but the way of the wicked leads them astray." "One who has unreliable friends soon comes to ruin, but there is a friend who sticks closer than a brother."

Our relationships reveal what's in our hearts in another way as well. *The effect we have* on people shows what kind of people we really are. "As iron sharpens iron, so one person sharpens another." "Walk with the wise and become wise, for a companion of fools suffers harm." When you're in a close relationship with another person, they begin to take on your character, and you take on theirs.

Just as the blessing of God is seen not in having a lot of money, but in having good money; and not in having a lot to say, but in having good things to say; so it's seen in not necessarily having a lot of friends (being "popular"), but in having good friends. It's a matter of quality, not quantity. Fake friends, who are only around for what they can get out of you, are a dime a dozen. "The poor are shunned even by their neighbors, but the rich have many friends."

⊃ If we want to be wise and "choose our friends carefully," how should we go about doing this? What qualities should we look for in a friend? What are the signs that someone would be a bad friend to have?

⊃ Think of someone who's been a good influence on you over the course of a close relationship. How has their character "rubbed off on you"? In what ways are you a better person because of their influence? Where are you beginning to have the same effect on other people yourself?

⊃ If you know someone who's been betrayed by "fake friends," tell what happened (without naming any names or revealing any identities). Once everyone who has a story to share has told it, see what general lessons you can draw from all of the stories.

2 A fourth area of life where our heart is revealed is in our reputation. This doesn't mean fame or celebrity. People can quickly achieve short-term notoriety for all kinds of things that have little to do with character. Rather, reputation is the way a person is regarded by the community of people who interact with them over a long period of time.

Character has a social footprint: "The crucible for silver and the furnace for gold, but people are tested by their praise."

In a society that judges by superficial, inborn characteristics such as appearance and talent, a person who isn't living in the fear of the LORD may initially achieve a very high "positive recognition factor," while a godly person may languish in obscurity. But sooner or later, what's really in a person's heart will be expressed in their actions. If these actions are unjust and destructive to other people, the person will get a bad reputation. By contrast, those who quietly but consistently do good may eventually be recognized and celebrated. "When wickedness comes, so does contempt, and with shame comes reproach." "When the righteous prosper, the city rejoices; when the wicked perish, there are shouts of joy."

Reputation, too, is a matter of quality, not quantity. What matters is not how many people have heard of you, but what the people who have heard of you think of you.

⮑ "A good name is more desirable than great riches; to be esteemed is better than silver or gold." Are there sometimes circumstances in life where we have to choose between "a good name" and "great riches"? Do you know someone who has a "good name" because they pursued honor and integrity even though it cost them money? Tell the group about them if you can. Can you give examples of people who've lost their "good name" because they went after "great riches" instead?

⮑ Think of someone whose public reputation has suddenly changed from good to bad. Where did they go wrong?

⮑ Do you know someone in a service or sales position (car dealer, auto mechanic, dry cleaner, etc.) who you'd recommend to a friend without hesitation? What qualities do they have that make you vouch for their reputation?

WHAT BRINGS THE CONTENT OF THE HEART OUT INTO KEY AREAS OF LIFE

Book of Proverbs > Solomon's Proverbs, continued

INTRODUCTION

So far we've seen that every person has a core of being, or "heart," that embodies who they truly are deep down inside. It's difficult to see directly into anyone's heart, but its character is revealed by how a person uses their money, what they say, who their friends are, and what their reputation is. In this session, we'll consider the specific means by which the content of the heart gets expressed in these areas of life.

READING

Take turns reading the next 50 proverbs in this collection, marking the ones that strike you and each sharing one or two of them at the end. Begin with "Each heart knows is own bitterness, and no one else can share its joy," and ending with "The path of life leads upward for the prudent to keep them from going down to the realm of the dead."

DISCUSSION

(For the following questions, and throughout this study guide, if any of the sayings you've been marking or recording for yourself sheds further light on the subjects being discussed, mention them to the group.)

1 According to Proverbs, what's in our heart works its way out into our life first through the "pleasure principle." We find it enjoyable and gratifying to do things that correspond with our heart's deepest intentions. "Fools find *pleasure* in wicked schemes, but those who have understanding *delight* in wisdom." "Folly brings *joy* to those who have no sense, but those who have understanding keep a straight course." "The wicked *crave* evil; their neighbors get no mercy from them."

This "pleasure principle" accounts for how our core-of-being gets expressed in the four specific areas of life we've been discussing. For example, it determines whether we speak "good words," or just many words: "Fools find no *pleasure* in understanding, but *delight* in airing their own opinions." It also determines who we will choose as friends: "The righteous *detest* the dishonest; the wicked *detest* the upright."

As we live our lives in the "fear of the LORD," our tastes actually change, so that wrong choices that were once pleasurable become undesirable, and right choices begin to attract us. The fourth opening speech in the book of Proverbs says, "If you accept my words and store up my commands within you . . . wisdom will enter your heart, and knowledge will be *pleasant* to your soul."

⮑ Based on the understanding you developed in session 3 of "good money" and "bad money," explain why a person living without regard for God would actually be attracted to "bad money" rather than to "good money."

⮑ Give group members a few moments to reflect on areas in their lives where their tastes have changed, so that wiser courses of action are now more appealing. As a group, pray together, both silently and aloud, thanking God for doing this work in your lives, and asking him to continue it.

2 What's in our hearts also gets expressed in our lives through the "return principle." God has set up the world so that whatever kinds of things, good or bad, we plan and prepare for others will come back into our own lives. "If anyone digs a pit, they themselves will fall into it; if anyone rolls a stone, it will roll back on them." (If you've seen the "Roadrunner" cartoons, think Wile E. Coyote here.) "Evil will never leave the house of one who pays back evil for good." "Whoever seeks good finds favor, but evil comes to those who search for it." Sooner or later, people always get a taste of their own medicine, whether bitter or sweet. You reap what you sow.

➲ Can you think of movies you've seen that accurately illustrate the "return principle," either by showing someone who's done good for others unpredictably receiving good things themselves, or by depicting a person who's plotted against others falling into trouble? Can you think of other movies that contradict the "return principle" and unrealistically show people who've done wrong to others living happily ever after?

3 Several other proverbs suggest that God sometimes acts more directly to make sure that good initiatives are rewarded and bad ones are thwarted. "The eyes of the LORD are everywhere, keeping watch on the wicked and the good." "Good people obtain favor from the LORD, but he condemns those who devise wicked schemes." "Trouble pursues the sinner, but the righteous are rewarded with good things." God will "repay everyone according to what they have done." This is the "payback principle." It's an expression of God's active justice in our world.

➲ Can you think of a situation you've seen or heard about in which a good initiative was "coincidentally" advanced by an unanticipated turn of events, or a bad initiative was unexpectedly thwarted?

4 Everything else being equal, these three principles will ensure that what's in a person's heart will find its way out into their life. People will experience the consequences, good or bad, of the choices their hearts lead them to make. However, Proverbs also tells us that this process will sometimes be divinely overruled. God may sovereignly decide to further his own purposes on earth despite what would otherwise happen because of what's in people's hearts. This is the "providential principle." "Many are the plans in a human heart, but it is the LORD's purpose that prevails." "There is no wisdom, no insight, no plan that can succeed against the LORD." "The LORD works out everything to its proper end."

This brings us back to the place where we reverently admit that there are some things that are just too profound for us to know. Even though following the path of wisdom may eventually help us reach great insights into our own hearts, God's inscrutable providence is always at work in the background. "A person's steps are directed by the LORD. How then can anyone understand their own way?"

⮑ Have you ever had an experience where you felt that God "saved you from yourself" by providentially overruling what would otherwise have been the consequences of your choices? Or have you seen God apparently intervene in some other way to accomplish his purposes, despite what people's hearts were leading them to do? If so, share your experience with the group if you can.

RECEIVING AND GIVING CORRECTION

INTRODUCTION

To this point, we've seen that what's in our hearts will inevitably be expressed in key areas of life: our finances, words, friendships, and reputation. We've seen that this happens through principles God has built into the way the world works: People find pleasure in doing things that match the intentions of their hearts; the good or bad that people try to send out into others' lives comes back into their own lives; God also intervenes directly to reward good courses of action and to thwart bad ones, and to fulfill his own purposes despite what people's hearts are leading them to do.

So if we want to have a good life, we need to have a good heart. How can our hearts be properly shaped and transformed? As we'll see in this session, there's a hard way, and an easier way.

READING

Take turns reading the next 50 proverbs in this collection, noting the ones that strike you. Begin with "The LORD tears down the house of the proud, but he sets the widow's boundary stones in place," and end with

"A bribe is seen as a charm by those who give it; they think success will come at every turn."

You'll notice a change after the first five proverbs in this session's reading. To this point in the "signature collection" of Solomon's proverbs, the second line of each saying has most often drawn a contrast with the first line. In the rest of the collection, the second line will typically restate the meaning of the first line, or extend that meaning in some way.

DISCUSSION

1 Proverbs tells us that one method of getting a better heart is to learn the hard way: by experiencing the painful consequences of making wrong choices, and recognizing that we need to change our values and priorities if we want to avoid further pain. In the third opening speech, Wisdom says to those who "did not choose to fear the LORD": "since you disregard all my advice and do not accept my rebuke, I in turn will laugh when disaster strikes you; I will mock when calamity overtakes you." We head in the wrong direction and suffer badly for it; we hear wisdom say "I told you so"; and perhaps we smarten up.

It's much better to learn the easy way: by taking wisdom's advice and accepting its correction in the first place. "Listen to advice and accept discipline, and at the end you will be counted among the wise." There's a huge store of practical experience, bequeathed by earlier generations, available for the taking in these collected sayings. "Come, eat my food," wisdom says in the last opening speech, "and drink the wine I have mixed. Leave your simple ways and you will live; walk in the way of insight."

People who give and receive correction can spare themselves and others a lot of heartache on the way to a good heart. "Whoever disregards discipline comes to poverty and shame, but whoever heeds correction is honored." "The wise in heart accept commands, but a chattering fool comes to ruin." "Whoever heeds discipline shows the way to life, but whoever ignores correction leads others astray."

⮱ Each of the following proverbs describes a source of correction and advice. Working together as a group, identify what each source is, and explain how guidance can be received from it. Then see if group members can give examples of dependable advice they've received from these sources.

- "A fool spurns a parent's discipline, but whoever heeds correction shows prudence."
- "My son, do not despise the LORD's discipline, and do not resent his rebuke, because the LORD disciplines those he loves, as a father the son he delights in."
- "Plans fail for lack of counsel, but with many advisers they succeed."
- "The teaching of the wise is a fountain of life, turning a person from the snares of death."

2 Because correction is such an important means of developing a good heart, Proverbs encourages us to offer correction and advice to others, as well as receiving it ourselves. Telling someone you think they're heading in the wrong direction is always difficult, and needs to be done with tact and good timing. But people should ultimately be grateful to receive cautionary advice: "Whoever rebukes a person will in the end gain favor rather than one who has a flattering tongue." "Wounds from a friend can be trusted, but an enemy multiplies kisses." It's not a good idea to offer unsolicited advice to people who don't want to hear it. But the better a person's heart, the more they will benefit from the insights of others. The last opening speech says, "Do not rebuke mockers or they will hate you; rebuke the wise and they will love you. Instruct the wise and they will be wiser still; teach the righteous and they will add to their learning."

⮱ Get volunteers in your group to act out the following situations. (They can fill in the details of the situation as they see fit.) After these three role-plays have been performed, discuss together what insights they've provided about how to offer correction wisely and effectively. As appropriate, make suggestions about what could have been done differently.

- A woman approaches one of her friends to warn her that the guy she's dating is hiding his prison record from her.
- A guy in college tells one of his buddies he's concerned about how much he's been drinking lately when they get together with their friends to watch sports.
- A business owner has given a summer job to the child of a friend, but needs to confront the young employee about being careless and chronically late for work.

3 Proverbs stresses often that one of the most important places to practice correction is in the family. Parents have a particular responsibility and a special opportunity to help shape their children's hearts from a young age. "Start children off on the way they should go, and even when they are old they will not turn from it." "Those who love [their children] are careful to discipline them."

⊃ If you have parents in your group, have them share one thing they've learned so far about how to shape godly hearts within their children through correction. Pray together as a group for these parents, that they will have wisdom, kindness, and patience for this important work.

CHARACTER QUALITIES:
THE FEAR OF THE LORD

INTRODUCTION

Proverbs seeks to give us a storehouse of wisdom that will serve as continual positive correction in our lives. This will shape our hearts so that we become people who are able to live out its moral and spiritual ideal. (As we've seen, not just anyone can do this; these proverbs are moral correction, not "simple, easy steps to success.")

The power for inner change comes from the work of God's Spirit in our hearts. But knowledge is also needed to show us where change has to take place, and to cut through the rationalizations we use to excuse our current way of living.

In practical terms, the reshaping of our hearts means that we develop essential character qualities. In the following sessions, we'll look at several of these qualities and discover how they can become the substance of our hearts. But first we'll explore a foundational quality that's the source of all the others: the "fear of the LORD."

READING

Take turns reading the next 50 proverbs in this collection, beginning with "Whoever would foster love covers over an offense, but whoever repeats the matter separates close friends," and ending with "Many curry favor with a ruler, and everyone is the friend of one who gives gifts." Each person should continue to note and share sayings that particularly speak to them.

DISCUSSION

1 Proverbs uses two different groups of terms to describe the person who's able to live out its moral and spiritual ideal. When it's focusing on the influences that have shaped this person's heart, it describes them with terms like "wise" and "prudent," as having things like "knowledge" and "insight." These terms contrast with the "fool," the "mocker," and so on—those who ignore or reject instruction. When the book is focusing on the way a person lives who's been shaped by these influences, it describes them with terms like "righteous" and "upright," by contrast with those who are "wicked," "sinners," "wayward," etc.

⮑ Look back over the proverbs you've marked or recorded so far. Note the ones that talk about the "wise" and "prudent" and those who have "insight" and "knowledge," as opposed to "fools" and "mockers." Also note the ones that describe the "righteous," "upright," etc. versus the "wicked," "sinners," "wayward," etc. What further insights can you get from these proverbs by knowing that they're talking about the same two kinds of people, just viewing them from different perspectives?

2 The foundational quality called the "fear of the LORD" is the source of all the other qualities of a *wise* person: "The fear of the LORD is the beginning of knowledge, but fools despise wisdom and instruction." The "fear of the LORD" is also the distinguishing characteristic of a *righteous* person: "Whoever fears the LORD walks uprightly, but those who despise him are devious in their ways."

What, then, is the fear of the LORD? It's a fundamental attitude of the heart. A person who fears the LORD doesn't dare do anything that would be displeasing to God. "Blessed are those who always *tremble before God*, but those who *harden their hearts* fall into trouble." In practical terms, to fear God means not doing anything we know is wrong. "To fear the LORD is to hate evil"; "through the fear of the LORD evil is avoided." Proverbs urges us to accept correction so that we can build this foundational quality into our hearts: "Do not be wise in your own eyes; fear the LORD and shun evil."

⮑ Often "fearing God" is explained as regarding God with reverence and respect, but not actually being afraid of him. However, the notion of not daring to do anything that's displeasing to God, of "trembling" before him, seems to suggest that we are afraid of what God might do to us, or let happen to us, if we do something wrong. Is it healthy to be "afraid" of God in this way? Why or why not? What other motives might a person have for not doing anything that would displease God?

⮑ In the next six sessions we'll look at some of the other character qualities that Proverbs encourages us to build into our lives. "Fearing the LORD" and not daring to do wrong will inevitably require us to cultivate these qualities and others like them. Divide your group into teams of two or three people, assign one of the qualities listed below to each team, and have them describe a scenario where a person who "feared the LORD" would have to develop this quality in order to avoid doing wrong.
- humility
- self-control
- diligence (hard work)

- caution (prudence)
- dependability (honesty, trustworthiness)
- justice

CHARACTER QUALITIES: HUMILITY

Book of Proverbs > Solomon's Proverbs, continued

INTRODUCTION

In the next several sessions, we'll look at specific character qualities that the "fear of the LORD," informed by wisdom and knowledge, and empowered by the Holy Spirit, builds into our lives. We'll begin in this session with an essential quality that ultimately decides whether a person will be wise or foolish, wicked or righteous, because it determines how willing a person is to receive correction. This is the quality of humility—it's the opposite of pride.

READING

Take turns reading the next 50 proverbs in the "signature collection" of Solomon's proverbs, beginning with "The poor are shunned by all their relatives—how much more do their friends avoid them!" and ending with "The human spirit is the lamp of the LORD that sheds light on one's inmost being."

DISCUSSION

1 The book of Proverbs ties the quality of humility directly to its major themes of character development. We've just seen that shaping a good heart begins by "fearing the LORD," that is, by not daring to do anything that displeases God. Several sayings, using some of the strongest language in the book, show how displeasing pride is to God. One of Solomon's proverbs says, "The LORD *detests* all the proud of heart. Be sure of this: They will not go unpunished." In the eighth opening speech, the first thing on the list of what "the LORD *hates*" is "haughty eyes" (a figure for an attitude of pride). In a later speech, wisdom says that "to fear the LORD is to hate evil" and then immediately adds, "I *hate* pride and arrogance."

➲ What is it about pride that makes God hate it so much?

2 We've seen that Proverbs describes a person whose heart has been shaped by correction and instruction as "wise," and that it describes that same person as "righteous" (as opposed to "wicked") when it's viewing them from the perspective of how they live. The book uses the language of both perspectives to warn against pride: "When pride comes, then comes disgrace, but with humility comes *wisdom*"; "Haughty eyes and a proud heart—the unplowed field of the *wicked*—produce sin."

Pride blocks the process that's designed to give us good hearts because it makes us unwilling to receive correction. We think we know better than anyone else and just do things our own way. "Where there is strife, there is pride, but wisdom is found in those who take advice." When, out of pride, we refuse to listen to advice, we fall into all the traps that godly friends and the wisdom of generations of God-fearing people could have warned us about, and we experience bitter consequences. "Pride goes before destruction, a haughty spirit before a fall." "Pride brings a person low, but the lowly in spirit gain honor."

➲ Without naming any names or revealing any identities, can you describe a situation where someone you know didn't listen to good advice because they were too proud? What happened to them?

⮑ Can you describe a situation when someone you know refused to listen to advice at first, but then humbled themselves and did what the wise counselors in their life were recommending? What happened in this situation?

3 Because pride, in the sense of arrogant self-sufficiency, is so deadly, it can't be given any place in our lives; it has to be "mortified" (killed off). One way to do this is by consistently practicing specific actions that express so much humility, pride can't survive them. Proverbs gives examples of humble behavior like this: "Do not exalt yourself in the king's presence, and do not claim a place among his great men; it is better for him to say to you, 'Come up here,' than for him to humiliate you before his nobles." "Let someone else praise you, and not your own mouth; an outsider, and not your own lips."

⮑ Describe what it would look like for someone today to follow the advice of the two proverbs just quoted.

⮑ What other genuinely humble actions would "mortify" pride? Choose one of them, try to put it into practice in the days ahead, and at your next session report how things went.

CHARACTER QUALITIES: SELF-CONTROL

Book of Proverbs > Solomon's Proverbs, concluded

INTRODUCTION

In this session you'll finish reading through the 375 proverbs in the "signature collection" of Solomon's sayings. In the discussion, you'll explore another character quality of a heart that's been shaped by wisdom: self-control.

Before you begin the reading and discussion, give group members the opportunity to report on the experiences they've had since your last session in "mortifying" pride.

READING

Take turns reading the final 50 proverbs in this collection, beginning with "Love and faithfulness keep a king safe; through love his throne is made secure," and ending with "Those who oppress the poor to increase their wealth and those who give gifts to the rich—both come to poverty."

After the reading, let group members share a few of their favorite proverbs from the entire collection.

DISCUSSION

1 Proverbs shows how important self-control is by illustrating it in several key areas of life. One of these is speech. "Those who guard their lips preserve their lives, but those who speak rashly will come to ruin."

Self-control in this area means, for one thing, not talking too much. "Those who have knowledge use words with restraint." "Even fools are thought wise if they keep silent, and discerning if they hold their tongues." It also means not talking too soon. "Do you see someone who speaks in haste? There is more hope for a fool than for them." "To answer before listening—that is folly and shame." "The heart of the righteous weighs its answers."

Self-control in speech also means not blurting out everything you know, but discerning what's appropriate to share in any given situation. "The prudent keep their knowledge to themselves, but a fool's heart blurts out folly." One of the most important ways to practice self-control in speech is by not gossiping. "Gossips betray a confidence, but the trustworthy keep a secret." "Gossips separate close friends." "Without wood a fire goes out; without a gossip a quarrel dies down."

➲ What other proverbs have you already noted that talk about self-control in speech? What do they teach us?

➲ In which of these ways have you seen a lack of self-control in speech harm relationships: talking too much; answering without thinking; revealing more than is appropriate; gossiping. (Share examples if you can—appropriately.) In which of these areas would you most like to have more self-control in your own speech?

◐ Who do you know who models good self-control in their speech? How do you think they're able to control what they say so well?

2 It's also vitally important for us to control our anger. Anger itself is simply an emotion; as such, it's morally neutral, neither right nor wrong. But it is wrong for us not to control our anger. When we lose our tempers, we regress morally. No matter how much wisdom and maturity we'd show under other circumstances, when we give in to anger, we act like fools. "The quick-tempered do foolish things"; "Fools give full vent to their rage." This unleashes the destructive effects of anger into our relationships: "An angry person stirs up dissension, and a hot-tempered person commits many sins."

Proverbs gives examples of a couple of traits that make people more prone to losing their tempers: being impatient and being easily offended. "Those who are patient have great understanding, but the quick-tempered display folly"; "Fools show their annoyance at once, but the prudent overlook an insult."

◐ What other traits or attitudes also make people more likely to lose their tempers? Under what circumstances might an ordinarily even-tempered person lose control of their anger?

◐ How can a person learn to "step back from the brink" and not let their anger rise to a level where it's bound to explode?

3 Proverbs also stresses the importance of self-control in eating and drinking. The sayings in the book come from an agricultural setting where resources were limited and uncertain. Overindulgence would lead directly to poverty, both by using up too many of a person's resources and by distracting them from the hard work needed to make a living: "Whoever loves pleasure will become poor; whoever loves wine and oil will never be rich." "Do not join those who drink too much wine or gorge themselves on meat, for drunkards and gluttons become poor, and drowsiness clothes them in rags." Conditions are still the same in many parts of the world today.

In more affluent countries, where food is abundant and affordable, eating and drinking too much doesn't usually lead directly to poverty (but it is linked to many serious health problems). But overconsumption of goods, purchased on credit, is still the ruin of many households that never learn to live within their means.

➲ Obesity has been identified as the #1 public health threat in affluent countries. The health problems associated with being overweight are actually causing these countries' average life expectancies to go down. Why are so many people in these countries so overweight? (What are the spiritual dimensions of the problem?)

➲ In less affluent countries today, what products or activities do people spend money on that they could otherwise use to have a better standard of living?

➲ Is it a form of gluttony to rack up so much credit card debt on consumer purchases that you can barely afford the minimum payments? Explain. If you know someone who's been able to pay off their credit cards after getting deeply into debt, share their story.

➲ In what other areas of life is it important to exercise self-control?

CHARACTER QUALITIES: DILIGENCE (HARD WORK)

INTRODUCTION

The next two collections in the book of Proverbs are "sayings of the wise." These collections are smaller, their authors and compilers are anonymous, and many of their sayings are several lines longer than Solomon's. Nevertheless, they continue to explain and illustrate the vision of life that's already been developed in the opening speeches and in the long collection of Solomon's proverbs.

In this session you'll begin reading the "sayings of the wise." In the discussion, you'll consider the character quality of diligence, or hard work. This quality is illustrated in the book of Proverbs by the contrast between the "diligent" person, who works hard and persistently, and the "sluggard" or lazy person, who avoids work and is always looking for an easy way out.

READING

Take turns reading the first 20 "sayings of the wise." The first is several lines long and begins, "Pay attention and turn your ear to the sayings of the wise"; the twentieth says, "Do not envy the wicked, do not desire their company; for their hearts plot violence, and their lips talk about making trouble." Continue to note and share the sayings that speak particularly to you.

(In *The Books of The Bible*, these sayings are set apart from each another by a little extra white space. In many other editions of the Bible, they have numbered headings. If your Bible doesn't have indications like these, stop when the subject changes; leave a brief pause before the next reader begins. Don't worry if you don't get the total to come out exactly to 20. There's a lot of thematic continuity between these sayings, so there's no harm in reading more than one of them at a time.)

DISCUSSION

1 The book of Proverbs paints a vivid portrait of the "sluggard," the person who will never amount to anything because they don't work hard to reach their goals. Some of the distinguishing characteristics of the sluggard (once again illustrated in an agricultural setting) are:

- They don't like to get out of bed. "As a door turns on its hinges, so a sluggard turns on the bed." (They're attached!) "Do not love sleep or you will grow poor; stay awake and you will have food to spare."
- They always have an excuse, often an outrageous one, for not working. "The sluggard says, 'There's a lion outside! I'll be killed in the public square!'" (if I try to go out to work). And there's no talking them out of it. "Sluggards are wiser in their own eyes than seven people who answer discreetly."
- They don't seize the moment. "Sluggards do not plow in season; so at harvest time they look but find nothing." "The lazy do not roast any game, but the diligent feed on the riches of the hunt."
- They're not motivated by the usual incentives for work. Ordinarily, "the appetite of laborers works for them; their hunger drives them on." In other words, people at least

work so they can meet their needs, and some of their wants. But "sluggards bury their hands in the dish and are too lazy to bring them back to their mouths." This is an overstatement, but it illustrates how "sluggards" aren't even motivated to meet their own basic needs.

• They're always trying to get rich quick through elaborate schemes that never pay off because these don't involve working hard to produce anything. "Those who work their land will have abundant food, but those who chase fantasies will have their fill of poverty." "All hard work brings a profit, but mere talk leads only to poverty."

➲ Have group members work in pairs to write short dialogues, set in today's world, that illustrate one of these characteristics of the "sluggard." The dialogue should take place between a sluggard and a diligent person. Have each pair read their dialogue for the group once it's written (or act it out improvisationally).

2 In addition to warning against the sluggard, sometimes through overstated parody, Proverbs also promises valuable rewards to the person who's diligent. "Lazy hands make for poverty, but diligent hands bring wealth." "Diligent hands will rule, but laziness ends in forced labor." "A sluggard's appetite is never filled, but the desires of the diligent are fully satisfied." "Do you see those who are skilled [diligent] in their work? They will serve before kings; they will not serve before officials of low rank."

➲ Reword each of the proverbs just quoted to bring it out of its ancient context—a world of kings and peasants—into your own culture. How would we express the same assurances of prosperity and promotion today?

⮕ How does diligence reflect the "fear of the LORD"? In other words, why is it displeasing to God if we don't work hard to reach our goals and fulfill our dreams?

⮕ Is it possible for a person to be too "diligent," in other words, to work too hard? How does a person know when they've worked "enough"? What's the difference between doing excellent, skilled work and trying to do everything perfectly?

CHARACTER QUALITIES: DEPENDABILITY

Book of Proverbs > Sayings of the Wise, continued
Book of Proverbs > More Sayings of the Wise

INTRODUCTION

In this session you'll read the rest of the "sayings of the wise," and also explore another characteristic of the heart that's shaped by the fear of the LORD. Proverbs speaks in many places of qualities like honesty, integrity, loyalty, truthfulness, and trustworthiness. All of these can be summed up by the term "dependability." A dependable person can be counted on to do and say what they're supposed to, at the right time and in the right way.

READING

Take turns reading the last 10 sayings in the first collection of "sayings of the wise," and the 5 sayings in the short collection that follows.

Begin with, "By wisdom a house is built, and through understanding it is established; through knowledge its rooms are filled with rare and beautiful treasures," and end with the warning against being a "sluggard" that concludes, "poverty will come on you like a thief and scarcity like an armed man."

DISCUSSION

1 In several places Proverbs uses the figure of the "messenger" to illustrate the importance of dependability. Ancient Israel had no telephones or internet, and there were no regular postal or delivery services. When people needed to conduct business at a distance, they had to do it through a "messenger." Since family and servants typically had regular duties they couldn't leave, messengers were often casual laborers, hired for the specific task of carrying information and transacting business on behalf of those who sent them. Much depended on how reliable the messenger was: "Like a snow-cooled drink at harvest time [the heat of the summer] is a trustworthy messenger to the one who sends him." "To send a message by the hands of a fool is like cutting off one's feet or drinking poison." The figure of the messenger in ancient Israel corresponds to anyone in our world today who's trusted by someone else to fulfill a specific task.

➲ Share an experience, if you've had one recently, when someone failed to fulfill the responsibilities they were entrusted with on your behalf. (For example, someone misplaced your application and it wasn't approved because it missed the deadline.) What caused this person to fail in their responsibility: Carelessness? Lack of information? Not taking things seriously? Something else?

➲ Think of an important task you were entrusted with that you fulfilled successfully. What obstacles did you have to overcome to complete it? Was there ever a time when you felt like giving up? How were you able to keep going?

➲ Reword this proverb using modern-day examples: "Those who guard a fig tree will eat its fruit, and those who protect their masters will be honored."

2 Another aspect of dependability is being someone your friends can count on to stand by them with help and good advice when they need you. "One who has unreliable friends soon comes to ruin, but there is a friend who sticks closer than a brother."

➲ Read each of the following proverbs and explain in your own words what characteristic of a dependable friend they're describing:
- "A friend loves at all times, and a brother is born for a time of adversity."
- "A gossip betrays a confidence; so avoid anyone who talks too much."
- "Wounds from a friend can be trusted, but an enemy multiplies kisses."
- "Perfume and incense bring joy to the heart, and the pleasantness of a friend springs from their heartfelt advice."

➲ Describe a time when a friend stood by you when you really needed them to.

3 Being dependable also means that other people can count on you to tell the truth. Proverbs draws a contrast between being loyal/trustworthy and telling lies: "What is desired in a person is loyalty [TNIV "unfailing love"]; better to be poor than a liar." "The LORD detests lying lips, but he delights in people who are trustworthy."

➲ You're about to hire a contractor to do some work on your house. He has excellent references, and you like the work he's done on some other houses. But as you're drawing up an agreement with him, you catch him in a lie. Are you still comfortable having him do the work for you?

(In this session, we've only been able to look at a few aspects of the related qualities that make up dependability: honesty, integrity, loyalty, trustworthiness, etc. As you've read through Proverbs, if you've noted other sayings that talk about this quality, share them with the group and discuss how they fill out the picture here.)

CHARACTER QUALITIES: CAUTION (PRUDENCE)

INTRODUCTION

There's a second collection of Solomon's sayings in the book of Proverbs. They were collected by "the men of Hezekiah king of Judah" about 250 years after Solomon lived. This shows how proverbs were passed down by word of mouth from generation to generation before being recorded in writing. As a tribute to this later king who valued Solomon's wisdom, the collection contains 130 proverbs, which reflects the numerical value of the Hebrew letters in Hezekiah's name.

This collection has two parts. The first 75 sayings show us another side of Solomon as a creator and collector of proverbs. These are often several lines long, and many of them develop figures of speech ("like cold water to a weary soul is good news from a distant land"). The last 55 proverbs in this collection are two-line sayings that describe the righteous and the wicked. In this session, you'll start reading the first part of this "Hezekiah collection."

In the discussion, you'll consider another character quality that the "fear of the LORD" builds into a person's heart: caution. This is often spoken of as "prudence" in Proverbs. It doesn't mean being hesitant to take decisive steps in life. (That's a characteristic of the sluggard instead.) Rather, caution or prudence means foresight: looking before you leap.

READING

Take turns reading the first 40 proverbs in this collection, beginning with "It is the glory of God to conceal a matter; to search out a matter is the glory of kings" and ending with, "Like one who grabs a stray dog by the ears is someone who rushes into a quarrel not their own."

DISCUSSION

1 Proverbs tells us that the cautious person examines a situation carefully, considering all of the intangibles, before committing to a course of action. "The wisdom of the prudent is to give thought to their ways." Because they fear God and acknowledge his sovereignty over the whole world, prudent people recognize that much in any situation will be beyond their control, so they make sure they're not exposed to unnecessary risks. They know when to get out of a situation that's shaping up badly. "The prudent see danger and take refuge, but the simple keep going and pay the penalty."

Prudence is opposed to haste, which is not taking the time to plan ahead, verify the facts, and think things through. "Desire without knowledge is not good—how much more will hasty feet miss the way." "The simple believe anything, but the prudent give thought to their steps." It's also the opposite of presumption, the attitude that says, "Whatever comes up, I know I can handle it." "The wise fear the LORD and shun evil, but a fool is hotheaded [impetuous] and yet feels secure."

➲ In which of the following ways would you like to be more prudent? Why? (Share, if you're free to, an experience where having been more prudent in this way would have helped you.)

    a. Looking over situations more carefully before committing yourself.

   b. Making sure you're not exposed to unnecessary risks.

   c. Not acting on desires without having the necessary information first.

   d. Not believing everything you're told without verifying it.

   e. Not assuming you can handle anything that comes up all by yourself.

⮑ Have you had an experience where a prudent person helped protect you from a threat or danger you couldn't foresee? If so, share it with the group.

2 Relationships are an area of life where Proverbs particularly stresses being prudent. "The righteous choose their friends carefully, but the way of the wicked leads them astray." This saying can be translated more literally, "A righteous person" (meaning someone whose life is shaped by the fear of the LORD) "is cautious in friendship." Prudent people recognize that their friendships will shape their own hearts and lives, and they carefully consider what kind of influence potential friends will have on them. "Do not make friends with the hot-tempered, do not associate with those who are easily angered, or you may learn their ways and get yourself ensnared."

⮑ Name a person you've been close to whose influence has shaped your character in a way you're grateful for. What made you want to get to know this person well? (This could be a relative as well as a friend: While we can't choose our relatives, we can choose which ones we become close to.)

3 Proverbs also describes a particular way of being prudent in our finances. "Put your outdoor work in order and get your fields ready; after that, build your house." "Be sure you know the condition of your flocks, give careful attention to your herds. . . . The lambs will provide you with clothing, and . . . you will have plenty of goats' milk to feed your family." In other words (to apply these sayings from an ancient agrarian culture to ourselves today), first make sure that you have a dependable source of income, and then take on only those expenses it enables you to afford.

➲ Does your society encourage people to be "prudent" like this with their finances? If you or someone you know follows specific financial practices and disciplines that you feel are "prudent," describe what they are.

CHARACTER QUALITIES: JUSTICE

Book of Proverbs > Hezekiah's Collection, Part 1, continued

INTRODUCTION

So far we've looked at several of the character qualities that Proverbs encourages us to build into our lives. The book promises that, everything else being equal, if we cultivate qualities like self-control, hard work, dependability, and prudence, our efforts will succeed, and we'll be prosperous and happy.

But Proverbs knows only too well that everything else is not equal. It notes that the world is full of wicked people who exploit and oppress others, depriving them of the fruit of their labors. "There are those . . . whose teeth are swords and whose jaws are set with knives to devour the poor from the earth and the needy from among humankind." "An unplowed field produces food for the poor, but injustice sweeps it away." So is there any point trying to live in the right way, if the wicked are just going to seize everything? Why suffer with the innocent when you could prosper with the ruthless?

Knowing that people will ask these questions, Proverbs emphasizes repeatedly that God is on the side of justice, not the side of injustice. God will defend the poor and defeat the wicked: "Do not exploit the poor because they are poor and do not crush the needy in court, for the LORD will take up their case and will exact life for life." So a distinguishing mark of godliness is to join in this work: "The righteous care about justice for the poor, but the wicked have no such concern." In this session we'll explore some of the ways Proverbs shows us we can be part of God's work of justice in the world.

You'll also continue reading Hezekiah's collection of sayings, which continues to speak to the many different topics addressed in the book as a whole.

READING

Take turns reading the next 35 proverbs in this collection. Begin with "Like a maniac shooting flaming arrows of death is one who deceives a neighbor and says, 'I was only joking!'" and end with the challenge to take care of one's flocks that concludes, "You will have plenty of goats' milk to feed your family and to nourish your women servants." Continue to note and share the sayings that speak particularly to you, and discuss in your group any proverbs that are unclear.

DISCUSSION

1 To work against injustice in the world, Proverbs stresses, first of all, show generosity and compassion to the poor, giving freely to help meet their needs. "Blessed are those who are kind to the needy." "The righteous give without sparing." This generosity is an expression of the "fear of the LORD," and God will bless it. "Whoever oppresses the poor shows contempt for their Maker, but whoever is kind to the needy honors God." "The generous will themselves be blessed, for they share their food with the poor."

➲ Silently consider how well you're living out these aspects of this character quality:
  • Being kind to the needy

- Giving generously, without sparing
- Giving in honor of God
- Other aspects you're aware of from other proverbs

What's one step you'd like to take to practice more generosity and compassion?

⊃ What organizations do you know that are effectively and reliably helping the poor in your community and around the world with needs such as food, water, clothing, shelter, and medicine? Give each person a chance to describe one or two organizations they're confident in supporting, and share about ways that others in the group can help with their current projects and initiatives. If anyone has had the opportunity to visit an organization's work on the field, let them tell about what they saw.

2 Another essential aspect of fighting injustice in the world is to practice justice in our own personal dealings with others. This means not cheating or taking advantage of the powerless. Proverbs warns specifically against several dishonest and exploitive practices of its time:

- Using lighter weights and smaller measures to give the poor less than their money's worth in trade, knowing that even if they recognize they're being cheated, they can't fight back. The book uses very strong language to oppose this practice: "The LORD *detests* dishonest scales, but accurate weights find favor with him." "Differing weights and differing measures—the LORD *detests* them both." God is on the side of justice in this matter: "Honest scales and balances belong to the LORD; all the weights in the bag are of his making."
- Moving boundary stones to deprive people of their land: "Do not move an ancient boundary stone set up by your ancestors." Once again, God is on the side of justice: "The

LORD tears down the house of the proud, but he sets the widow's boundary stones in place."

- Driving prices up by limiting supply: "People curse those who hoard grain, but they pray God's blessing on those who are willing to sell."

➲ In your own society, what are some of the ways that one person might try to cheat or exploit another person? (For example, by turning back the odometer on a used car.) What remedies are available to people who think they've been cheated? Can everyone use these remedies equally effectively? If not, who advocates for those who can't?

➲ Today we live in a truly globalized economy, so that the choices we make to buy products and use resources affect the lives of people in other parts of the world, even if we never interact with them face to face. If you or a group you belong to (such as your church) is doing something to promote greater justice through what you purchase and use, tell the group about it.

3 In addition to compassion for the needy and fair dealing between individuals, Proverbs stresses the need for society-wide justice. The entire society needs to be governed by fair and honest standards, obeyed and enforced by those in power. When a country is run by wicked and corrupt people, it falls apart. But when justice prevails, there is long-term stability.

The sayings in the book of Proverbs were created and collected at a time when countries were ruled by kings who were also the highest judicial authorities in the land. Solomon and Hezekiah, as kings, maintained justice in their own realms, and their collections of proverbs contain many admonitions for their fellow kings to do right so they can have long, stable reigns. "Remove wicked officials from the king's presence, and his throne will be established through righteousness." "If a king judges the poor with fairness, his throne will be established forever." "By justice a king gives a country stability, but those who are greedy for bribes tear it down."

⮑ Where in the world today do we see societies destabilized and disintegrating because their rulers are trying to hang on to power through corruption?

⮑ Many countries today no longer have a single, all-powerful, leader-for-life. Instead, power is divided up among various branches of government, and elections and term limits keep people from staying in office. In this more complex situation, society-wide justice depends on the collective efforts of all citizens, not just the character of the ruler. What are some specific ways that those who "fear the LORD" can help ensure justice throughout their societies today?

WARNINGS AGAINST DRUNKENNESS AND SEXUAL IMMORALITY

Book of Proverbs > Hezekiah's Collection, Part 2

INTRODUCTION

Over the past few sessions we've looked at several character qualities that reflect the "fear of the LORD." Proverbs has much more to say about these qualities and others like them, but it's not possible to consider all of its extensive wisdom within this short study guide. Hopefully this introduction to the book will encourage you to revisit its sayings over and over again in the years ahead.

In the next two sessions we'll conclude our consideration of Proverbs by looking at the warnings it gives about several traps that people commonly fall into in life. These are serious mistakes that are easy to make if we're inexperienced and not yet trained in wisdom. They can ruin our lives before we ever have the chance to live in the "fear of the LORD." To protect and preserve us so we can follow the path of character development, Proverbs sounds clear warnings about these traps. Yes, you have to chart the right course in life, but you also have to watch out for anything that might sink the ship.

READING

Finish reading the "proverbs of Solomon compiled by the men of Hezekiah." The last 55 proverbs in this collection are two-line sayings that describe the righteous and the wicked. The first, middle, and last of these sayings draw a direct contrast between the two.

Read the opening proverb in the second part of this collection out loud together as a group: "The wicked flee though no one pursues, but the righteous are as bold as a lion."

Then take turns reading the 26 proverbs that follow, ending with "Those who give to the poor will lack nothing, but those who close their eyes to them receive many curses."

As a group, read the middle proverb together: "When the wicked rise to power . . ."

Take turns reading the next 26 proverbs, ending with "Many seek an audience with a ruler . . ."

Finally, read the last proverb aloud together: "The righteous detest the dishonest; the wicked detest the upright."

DISCUSSION

1 One of the things that Proverbs warns can "sink the ship" is getting drunk. "Wine is a mocker and beer a brawler; whoever is led astray by them is not wise." "Do not gaze at wine when it is red, when it sparkles in the cup, when it goes down smoothly! In the end it bites like a snake and poisons like a viper." A person who's had too much to drink is not in command of their senses. They can easily be led astray into unwise and unjust actions. For example, in light of the concern for justice we explored in our last session, "It is not for kings to drink wine, not for rulers to crave beer, lest they drink and forget what has been decreed, and deprive all the oppressed of their rights." Chronic drunkenness also destroys a person's productivity and health. "Do not join those who drink too much wine . . . for drunkards . . . become poor, and drowsiness clothes them in rags." (If Proverbs were written today, it would also warn against getting high on drugs, since this has these same effects.)

⮕ What kinds of life-ruining mistakes can a person make who gets drunk or high, even if they only do so occasionally and aren't an alcoholic or drug addict? If the potential consequences are so serious, why do people still use drugs and alcohol recreationally? What can help a person give up this behavior?

⮕ Do you know anyone who's become addicted to drugs or alcohol? How has this affected their relationships and work? Have they been able to recognize their need for help, and get it? If so, what are some of the keys to their ongoing recovery? Have you been able to help them personally?

2 Another warning that Proverbs sounds very clearly is against sexual immorality. At the time the book was written, this primarily took the form of adultery, meaning in this culture sexual relations between a man (married or single) and someone else's wife. In ancient Israel, young women were married around the age of 14, as soon as they were able to have children. Until then, they lived in their father's homes. So premarital sex was not common. But, as the warnings in the book show, some young married women tried to attract lovers who would give them adventure, money, and gifts. "Adultery" in this case was only a step removed from prostitution.

The opening speeches in the book offer several extended warnings against adultery. Because they are addressed from fathers to sons, they caution against being seduced by a "wayward woman." This, they warn, will lead to being "taken" for a lot of money or to being punished severely by a jealous husband. "Do not go near the door of her house . . . lest strangers feast on your wealth and your toil enrich the house of another." "Jealousy arouses a husband's fury, and he will show no mercy when he takes revenge."

However, this doesn't mean that Proverbs depicts women as entirely to blame for sexual immorality. There are other warnings throughout the book for men to control their own eyes and desires: "Do not lust in your heart after her beauty" (speaking of the adulteress). Men are told to be faithful to their own marriage vows: "Rejoice in the wife of your youth . . . may you ever be intoxicated with her love."

Having sexual relations only within marriage is an expression of the "fear of the LORD." The adulterous woman "has left the partner of her youth and ignored the covenant she made before God. . . . None who go to her . . . attain the paths of life."

➲ Give some recent examples of well-known, successful people who've been publicly disgraced because they had sexual relations outside of marriage. What did this cost them? Why do people who have so much to lose risk it all by having these affairs?

➲ What are the destructive effects on people's lives of other forms of sexual immorality that are more common in our day than they were in the time of Proverbs, such as premarital sex and pornography? How can people keep from getting caught up in these activities?

WARNINGS AGAINST GANGS AND PUTTING UP SECURITY

Book of Proverbs > Sayings of Agur
Book of Proverbs > Sayings of King Lemuel

INTRODUCTION

The book of Proverbs concludes with two short collections of sayings by men named Agur and Lemuel. We don't know anything else about them, but it's clear they shared a common vision, for a life lived in the fear of God, with Solomon and the "wise" whose sayings are collected in the rest of the book. (The description of "a wife of noble character" at the very end of the book may come from yet another writer. It's an independent composition, a poem whose 22 lines begin with the consecutive letters of the Hebrew alphabet.)

In this session we'll finish reading through the book, and also conclude our thematic consideration by looking at two more warnings it gives about common traps that people fall into.

READING

Take turns reading the sayings of Agur.

Then have one person read the first part of the "sayings of King Lemuel," up to "defend the rights of the poor and needy." Have another person read the description of "a wife of noble character."

DISCUSSION

1 Just as the opening speeches offer several long warnings against adultery, they also caution at length against becoming part of gangs. In fact, this is the very first specific topic addressed in the book: "If sinful men entice you, do not give in to them. If they say, 'Come along with us; let's lie in wait for innocent blood . . .'—my son, do not go along with them, do not set foot on their paths." Later speeches extend the warning: "Wisdom will save you from the ways of wicked men . . . who have left the straight paths to walk in dark ways."

One strong attraction of these gangs is that, through criminal activity, members can quickly get a lot more wealth than they could get honestly. They also get a strong sense of belonging. "We will get all sorts of valuable things and fill our houses with plunder," the gang recruiters promise, "we will all share the loot." But members will also be expected to support the gang with all of their own future "takings," as well as through violence. It's likely, Proverbs warns, that they may ultimately pay with their own lives: "Such are the paths of all who go after ill-gotten gain; it takes away the life of those who get it."

⊃ How active are gangs where you live? How organized are they: are they loose, informal groups or local branches of national gangs? (If you're not sure, check with some teenagers you know.) What draws a person into a formal or informal gang? What kinds of things happen to people who get involved in gangs that can destroy their futures? What are the most effective ways of encouraging people not to join gangs, or to leave them if they have joined?

2 Another repeated warning in the book of Proverbs is against putting up security for another person, particularly for a stranger. Ancient Israel did not have an extensive system of financing and credit such as we have today. A person who incurred a financial obligation but didn't have the confidence of the lender had to get the backing of someone in the community who would agree to meet the obligation if they defaulted. This person would shake hands with the lender to pledge their own resources to back the debt. (The modern equivalent is co-signing a loan for another person.)

Proverbs warns that it's foolish and risky to do this for someone you don't know: "Whoever puts up security for a stranger will surely suffer, but whoever refuses to shake hands in pledge is safe." "Do not be one who shakes hands in pledge or puts up security for debts; if you lack the means to pay, your very bed will be snatched from under you."

➲ A charitable organization that your mother has long supported wants to acquire some property and build a new building. Because most of its income is from voluntary donations, the bank that's offering a mortgage asks it to have a number of its supporters co-sign the loan. The signers will be "jointly and severally liable," meaning that if the organization defaults, the bank can collect the entire debt from all of them together, or from any one of them. Your mother has been asked to co-sign, and she asks your advice about what to do. What do you tell her?

➲ The basic principle behind the warning against putting up security is that we shouldn't put our finances at risk by making them vulnerable to the actions of people we don't know and can't control. In what other ways, besides co-signing loans, do we do this in our world today? Do you know anyone who's been ruined financially because they risked too much of this kind of exposure? Is a certain amount of risk justified by potential returns? If so, what safeguards can a person put in place to protect against excessive losses?

3 You've now read all the way through the book of Proverbs, and also considered its major themes:

- The "heart" as the core of being
- The way what's in our "heart" is expressed in our words, use of money, relationships, and reputation
- The principles that draw what's in our heart out into these spheres of life: pleasure, "return," God's justice, and God's sovereignty
- How our hearts can be shaped the "easier way" by giving and receiving correction
- The character qualities of a good heart, all rooted in the "fear of the LORD"
- Common traps in life that can "sink the ship" before our hearts are shaped

⊃ Give everyone in the group the chance to share two or three main things they've gotten out of this study of Proverbs, and what they've learned about themselves and about life.

In the next session, you'll begin reading and discussing another biblical book in the wisdom tradition, Ecclesiastes. It's similar to Proverbs in many ways, but it's written in a slightly different style, and it speaks from a complementary perspective about how to live well on this earth.

ECCLESIASTES

EXPERIENCING THE BOOK OF ECCLESIASTES AS A WHOLE

Book of Ecclesiastes (Overview)

INTRODUCTION

Read this introduction aloud in your group and give people a chance to ask questions about it before reading through Ecclesiastes together.

Ecclesiastes is another book in the Bible that comes from the wisdom tradition. It has many similarities to Proverbs: It presents short sayings that are the distilled wisdom of experience, and it considers the wise and foolish ways of life in order to advise how best to live in this world. But there's a significant difference: while Proverbs contains collections of sayings that are meant to be engaged one at a time, Ecclesiastes is a single extended discourse with individual sayings woven into it. So it's appropriate to begin our consideration of Ecclesiastes by experiencing it all at once, which we'll do in this session.

Because the author of Ecclesiastes is called the "son of David, king in Jerusalem," he's often identified with Solomon. However, within the book, he prefers to be known simply as "the Teacher." He's given this title at the beginning and end of the book. Many interpreters understand it to mean that he was someone who addressed an assembly, or gathered people together to hear his wisdom, because this title "Teacher" (*Qoheleth*) is derived from the Hebrew word for an assembly or gathering (*qahal*). (The name of the book, Ecclesiastes, is a Greek translation of this Hebrew title *Qoheleth*.)

While Ecclesiastes contains proverbs and poems, it's largely made up of a series of "reflections." The reflection is an approach to wisdom teaching that typically begins by making an observation and then considering it from various perspectives. In the process, proverbs may be quoted to bring in different insights. Finally, a conclusion is drawn; these conclusions often express judgments: "it is good to . . ." or "better is this . . . than that." (Some reflections don't proceed this systematically, but they still present these same elements of observation, consideration, and conclusion.) Here's a brief example of one of the book's "reflections." In it, both the consideration and the conclusion consist of single proverbs:

Observation	I saw that all toil and all achievement spring from one person's envy of another. This too is meaningless, a chasing after the wind.
Consideration	Fools fold their hands and ruin themselves.
Conclusion	Better one handful with tranquillity than two handfuls with toil and chasing after the wind.

In other words, reflecting on his observation, the Teacher considers that if people don't do at least some work, they won't have enough to live on. But he concludes that envy shouldn't make them work so hard that their lives become just restless striving. (This example illustrates another distinguishing feature of Ecclesiastes: Sayings may be matched against one another to provide a well-rounded perspective. In Proverbs, as we've noted, sayings usually stand on their own.)

As the discourse unfolds, the shorter (minor) reflections in Ecclesiastes are gathered up to form longer (major) reflections. Each of these leads to the same overall conclusion, which is repeated seven times in the course of the book: "there is nothing better for people than to eat and drink and find satisfaction in their toil." We'll explore the meaning of this conclusion in the sessions ahead. While this larger "reflection" pattern provides a loose structure for the book, the discourse is nevertheless intentionally repetitive, almost rambling, alternating between poetry and prose. This form is designed to mirror the book's description of life, which it symbolizes in its opening speech by the wind that goes "round and round, ever returning on its course."

As you listen to Ecclesiastes, you'll frequently hear the word "meaningless," translating the Hebrew term *hebel*. (It occurs 37 times in the book*—equaling the numerical value of the letters in the word *hebel*.) It's important to understand how this term is being used. It doesn't indicate "meaningless" in the modern, existential sense of life being absurd and having no sense or purpose other than what we bring to it. Rather, this Hebrew word describes something that is fleeting, temporary, precarious, and uncertain. It literally means a "mist" or "vapor," such as the mist that appears in the morning and quickly burns off in the sun. The word *hebel* is used in this literal sense in Proverbs: "A fortune made by a lying tongue is a fleeting *vapor*." When used more figuratively, *hebel* refers to anything that doesn't last, as when Proverbs says, "Charm is deceptive, and beauty is *fleeting*; but a woman who fears the LORD is to be praised." In one place within Ecclesiastes itself, the term appears to have this specific meaning: "You who are young, be happy while you are young . . . for youth and vigor are [fleeting]." But by inference, if something is uncertain or won't last, it can't be a reliable source of meaning in life, and this is the sense in which the term is most often used in Ecclesiastes. So when you hear "meaningless," understand this to indicate something that's "not a reliable source of enduring meaning."

Ecclesiastes is looking specifically at what happens "under the sun," that is, on this earth. It deliberately limits its perspective in order to challenge people who are living only for this life. It exposes how temporary

---

* Most interpreters agree that a 38th occurrence, "all the days of this meaningless life that God has given you under the sun—*all your meaningless days*," is an accidental duplication that arose during the copying process. It's not found in many early Greek and Aramaic versions of the book.

and uncertain rewards like wealth and reputation are, to encourage people to live for things that are more enduring. This is another difference between Ecclesiastes and the book of Proverbs. Proverbs promises wealth, reputation, good friends, and gracious, influential speech as the rewards of a heart reshaped by the "fear of the LORD." Ecclesiastes agrees that it's valuable to pursue wisdom, and that it leads to these things, but it warns urgently against pursuing them as ends in themselves—not in a world like this one, where all such rewards are uncertain and precarious, because "the race is not to the swift or the battle to the strong, nor does food come to the wise or wealth to the brilliant or favor to the learned; but time and chance happen to them all."

READING

Read through the book of Ecclesiastes out loud. This will take about 45 minutes. (It's on pages 1179–93 in *The Books of The Bible*. If you're using another edition, you should find it right after the book of Proverbs.) During the reading you can see how the book unfolds by following the chart on page 82.

Each person can read as much or as little as they'd like and then let the next person take their turn. (You may want to read just a poetical section, or just a prose section, and stop when the kind of writing changes.)

As you listen to the book, note how the discourse is punctuated by poems and proverbs, and try to recognize the shorter "reflections" by how they offer observations, considerations, and conclusions, usually (but not always) in that order. Also notice the seven larger conclusions, which all say how good it is for people to "eat and drink and find satisfaction in their toil," or similar words to that effect.

As you read the book aloud together, picture yourselves sitting in a group back in ancient Israel that has gathered together to hear this Teacher, listening to him as he spins out his thoughts and punctuates his discourse with clusters of short sayings.

DISCUSSION

⊃ Had you ever read Ecclesiastes before? If so, how was your experience of the book different this time through? If you'd never heard Ecclesiastes before, what were your first impressions?

⊃ What were your favorite parts of the book? What sayings did you like, and what perspectives did you appreciate? What didn't you like about the book? Were there some sayings that really bothered you? (If so, make a note of them, and ask your group to discuss them when you get to the session that explores the part of the book where they appear.)

⊃ Based on what you've discovered in this session, how would you answer someone who asked you, "So, what's the book of Ecclesiastes about?"

OUTLINE OF THE BOOK OF ECCLESIASTES

Title
"The words of the Teacher . . ."

Theme Statement:
"'Meaningless! Meaningless!' says the Teacher. . . . 'Everything is meaningless.'"

Poem:
"Generations come and generations go . . ."

First Major Reflection
Contains shorter reflections that end, "This is meaningless, a chasing after the wind."

Poem:
"There is a time for everything . . ."

Second Major Reflection

Third Major Reflection

Fourth Major Reflection
Contains shorter reflections that begin, "I saw . . . under the sun"

Fifth Major Reflection
Contains shorter reflections that end, "no one can discover/who can discover?"

Sixth Major Reflection

Seventh Major Reflection
Contains shorter reflections that end, "No one knows/you do not know"

Poem:
"Remember your Creator . . ."

Theme Statement:
"'Meaningless! Meaningless!' says the Teacher. 'Everything is meaningless!'"

Epilogue
"Not only was the Teacher wise . . ."

Major reflections all culminate in the same conclusion:
"It is good for people to eat and drink and find satisfaction in their toil."

INSIGHTS FROM EXPERIENCE

INTRODUCTION

Right after its opening title, Ecclesiastes makes its theme statement. It's the provocative assertion that will recur throughout the book: "Everything is meaningless." That is, none of the things people typically wear themselves out for actually provide enduring meaning and satisfaction in this life. The book then rephrases this thought in the form of a question: "What does anyone gain from all their labors at which they toil under the sun?" The implication of this question is, "Before you work really hard to get something, you need to ask yourself whether the payoff is going to be worth it." The rest of the book will demonstrate that, for most of the goals people pursue, it won't necessarily be worth it.

Once the overall theme has been announced, the extended discourse of the book begins, with a poem. It's a meditation on the natural world, describing the futility of making original achievement and lasting fame one's goals in life.

A series of five short "reflections" follows. The conclusion in each one is that life on earth (life "under the sun" or "under the heavens") is "a chasing after the wind"—that is, a hopeless pursuit of things we can never ultimately attain. But these five reflections are then gathered up into a larger (major) reflection by the introduction of a more positive conclusion: "People can do nothing better than to eat and drink and find satisfaction in their toil [work]. This . . . is from the hand of God." This same conclusion will reappear at intervals throughout the book and point the way to a more satisfying and meaningful life "under the sun."

READING

Have someone read the book's title, and then the opening assertion and question that express its overall theme.

Have someone else read the poem that comes next, beginning with, "Generations come and generations go, but the earth remains forever."

Then have five different people read the reflections. They begin:
- "I, the Teacher, was king over Israel in Jerusalem."
- "I said to myself, 'Look, I have grown and increased in wisdom . . .'"
- "I said to myself, 'Come now, I will test you with pleasure . . .'"
- "Then I turned my thoughts to consider wisdom, and also madness and folly" (ending, "All of it is meaningless, a chasing after the wind").
- "I hated all the things I had toiled for under the sun . . ." (ending, "This too is meaningless, a chasing after the wind").

DISCUSSION

1 The opening poem in the book of Ecclesiastes uses the natural world, where the sun, the wind, and the water move in endless cycles, to illustrate that there's really no originality or lasting renown in human culture—only repetition, which wipes out the memory of what came before. "There is nothing new under the sun"; "There is no remembrance of people of old, and even those who are yet to come will not be remembered by those who follow them."

⮑ For how many years into the future would you like your achievements to be recognized and remembered?

⮑ If any artistic, cultural, or technical achievement is bound to be, in some sense, only a repetition of something that's already been done, what incentive do people have to try to do really creative things?

2 The first two short reflections in this section don't follow the typical sequence of observation-consideration-conclusion. Instead, the conclusions are expressed first, and then the observations they're based on are stated:

- All the things that are done under the sun are meaningless . . . *because* what is crooked cannot be straightened, and what is lacking cannot be counted.
- Understanding wisdom, madness and folly is a chasing after the wind *because* with much wisdom comes much sorrow, and the more knowledge, the more grief.

These observations could be paraphrased this way:

- No matter how you live, you're always going to find that there's something missing here on this earth.
- People are happier and better off if they have naïve, unrealistic ideas about how life works.

⮑ Get volunteers from your group to form teams of two or three people to debate the "pro" and "con" of the two observations above, in their paraphrased form. (People can argue for a position even if they're not entirely convinced it's correct.) Give the teams a few minutes to prepare their arguments, then let each one present its side of the question for up to five minutes. Afterwards, give both teams a couple of minutes to rebut the other side. The remaining group members can vote on who won.

3 The core of this long reflection is the Teacher's description of how he pursued what he thought was worthwhile and rewarding in life, and what he learned as a result. He acquired great wealth and possessions, undertook a variety of interesting projects, and indulged in the pleasures and diversions that life has to offer. In the process, he earned a reputation as one of his nation's greatest kings. But in the end, he discovered that none of this was really worth living for, in and of itself.

The Teacher recognized, first of all, that nothing he'd worked for would last for a long time into the future: "When I surveyed all that my hands had done and what I had toiled to achieve, everything was meaningless" (*hebel*: fleeting, transient, temporary). He also observed that even though he had lived well—responsibly and creatively—his life would end, from an earthly perspective, just like the lives of those who had been foolish and wasted their abilities. Everyone, no matter how they've lived, eventually grows old, declines in health, and dies. And the teacher also realized, to his horror, that after his death everything he'd worked for would be put in the hands of someone who might be wise, but who might also be foolish and squander his accumulated wealth and tarnish his legacy.

In short, the Teacher concludes, it makes no sense to work hard all the time—and not enjoy life in the present—for the sake of what you believe will happen in the future *on the earth*. No matter how great your achievements and reputation, you're going to die in the end. And no matter how long your accomplishments last after you're gone, ultimately they'll disappear and you'll be forgotten. And so, he says, a person should live instead for what's happening in the present: They should find work that they will enjoy *while they're doing it*. (This is "incidental pleasure," not pleasure pursued as an end in itself, as the source of meaning in life.) The Teacher discovered that his own projects were a source of joy for him while he was working on them: "My heart took delight in all my labor, and this was the *reward* for all my toil." This answers the question that the book opens with: "What does anyone gain [what is anyone's *reward*] from all their labors at which they toil under the sun?" Experiencing this enjoyment in the present is something that can never be taken away from you, no matter what happens to your achievements in the future.

⮑ Based on this reflection, how would you answer someone who said:

- "I really don't like my job, and I have to work a lot of hours, but at least I'm setting myself up for a great retirement."
- "I've sacrificed a lot in terms of relationships, hobbies, and even my health, but I'm building a great institution that my successors will guide for many generations into the future."
- "God put us on this earth to work. We'll have plenty of time to rest in heaven."

⮑ Is it ever an appropriate *short-term* strategy to postpone *some* present enjoyment for the sake of anticipated future rewards? (For example, studying hard and working long hours to become a doctor, or working 80 to 100 hours a week for a couple of years right after college to pay off loans.) Once a person has achieved a significant goal like this, how can they shift gears and find a better balance between working towards further goals and enjoying life in the present? Do you know someone who's been able to do this effectively?

⮑ What do you think the Teacher would say about the proverbs that advocate diligence and warn against being a sluggard? Based on your study of Proverbs, and of Ecclesiastes to this point, how would you respond to someone who said, "I enjoy playing music (or acting, or playing sports, etc.), and if I can't make enough money at that to support a family, I'll just live with my parents, because I'm not going to waste my life working at some boring job just to pay the bills."

INSIGHTS FROM OBSERVATION

Book of Ecclesiastes > Second, Third, and Fourth Major Reflections

INTRODUCTION

The first major reflection in the book of Ecclesiastes was based primarily on what the Teacher learned from his own *experience*. After that reflection reaches its conclusion, the book restarts with another poem. It then restates its overall question ("What do workers gain from their toil?"). It then offers another series of shorter reflections that are now based on what the Teacher has *observed* about life. Instead of being introduced by accounts of his own experiences, most of these reflections begin with him saying "I *saw*" a certain thing "under the sun."

In this part of the book the overall conclusion, that it's good for people to eat and drink and find satisfaction in their work, is repeated three times. The first two times it comes after single reflections that are relatively brief, perhaps to emphasize this important conclusion right after it's first been stated. The third time, the conclusion comes, as it does more typically in other parts of the book, after a number of different reflections on various subjects. It pulls them all together into another major reflection as this observation-based portion of the book draws to a close.

READING

Have someone read the poem that introduces this next part of the book, beginning, "There is a time for everything, and a season for every activity under the heavens." This person should also read the conclusion that follows, ending, "God will call the past to account."

Then have different people read the reflections in this part of the book. They begin:

- "And I saw something else under the sun."
- "Again I looked and saw all the oppression that was taking place under the sun."
- "And I saw that all toil and all achievement spring from one person's envy of another."
- "Again I saw something meaningless under the sun."
- "Better a poor but wise youth than an old but foolish king . . ."
- "Guard your steps when you go to the house of God."
- "If you see the poor oppressed in a district, and justice and rights denied . . ."
- "I have seen a grievous evil under the sun."
- "This too is a grievous evil" (ending, "They seldom reflect on the days of their lives, because God keeps them occupied with gladness of heart").

DISCUSSION

1 The eloquent poem that begins this part of the book is an extended illustration of the truth that's stated at its conclusion: God has made everything beautiful (or "appropriate") in its time. That is, God knows that there are right times and seasons in our lives for both difficult and refreshing experiences, for the destruction of old things and the creation of new ones. But we don't know why this is so, and we also don't know why a given time is right for one thing rather than for another. This is one part of the "burden God has laid on the human race." The other part is that while we are time-bound, "eternity" has been set in our hearts. We know that what we do in this life is *significant* beyond this life, but we can't *see* beyond this life to understand exactly why or how. And so the Teacher advises, once again, that the best we can do is enjoy God's good gifts in the present (represented by "eating and drinking") and find work that's enjoyable and satisfying *while we're doing it*. In a paradoxical way, having this authentic experience of the present is somehow the surest way to know that our lives are also counting for eternity.

⮕ Give group members a few minutes to read through the poem and identify one or more "times" that they're living in right now. They can take the terms either literally or figuratively. (For example, someone might decide that in this season of their life, it's a "time to mourn," because they've lost a loved one; it's a "time to throw away," because they've been simplifying their possessions; and it's a "time to speak," because they need to address some things that have been going on in their workplace.) Those who are comfortable doing so can share one or more of the "times" they've identified. Pray together, silently and out loud, that God would show each person why it's appropriate for them to be in this "time" right now, or at least give them the assurance that it is.

2 The next reflection pursues the idea that people are time-bound but are nevertheless always looking beyond time. The Teacher is distressed to see how much unresolved injustice there is in the world. He concludes that God must execute judgment on the righteous and the wicked beyond this life. This is the only way to reconcile our moral sense and our understanding of God's character with the facts that we observe "under the sun."

In the second part of this reflection, the Teacher explains how God "tests" human beings by confronting them with the reality of physical death and the impossibility of knowing what follows. The word translated "test" here carries the notion of selecting or choosing. God is paradoxically calling out humanity from among the animals by provoking them with the insight that physically they're just like the animals—they're mortal. People's refusal to accept that death will be the end of them points them beyond this lifetime to their eternal destiny. But their inability to know for certain that they'll live on after death is their "burden" on earth. The solution, once again, is to find joy and satisfaction in the work we do here and now—we can count on that, at least.

⮑ Even if you have a strong faith in an afterlife, consider the Teacher's question here, which is intended to challenge people who are "so heavenly minded they're no earthly good": Who knows (for certain) whether people really live on after death? If you took the Teacher's question to heart, and decided to treat an afterlife not as something you could be certain about, even though it was something you could still legitimately have faith in, do you think this would lead you to treat this world as if it mattered more?

3 Just as it would take well over a decade to consider in depth each of the individual sayings in Proverbs, it would take far longer than this study guide can permit to consider each of the individual sayings and reflections in Ecclesiastes. Hopefully this guide will encourage you to return to the wisdom teaching of both books frequently in the years ahead. And it will be possible to consider many of the shorter reflections. The questions that follow provide some ways to get into the ones in this section; choose the ones that are most interesting to your group.

⮑ In your life right now, are you pursuing "two handfuls with toil," or "one handful with tranquility"? What would have to change if you decided that one handful, with tranquility, was better than two with toil?

⮑ How would you answer the question that the man without any family, who's just trying to make more and more money, finally asks himself: "For whom am I toiling, and why am I depriving myself of enjoyment?"

⮑ After questioning twice whether anyone really gains anything from their toil, the Teacher acknowledges that "two are better than one, because they have a good return for their labor." According to this passage, and in your own experience, how does the "work" of investing in a relationship pay off?

⮑ The Teacher says we shouldn't be surprised how little the poor have to show for their labors, because a whole line of officials, right up to the king, is skimming off their crops. Based on what you've heard in the rest of the book, do you think he's saying we just have to resign ourselves to this?

⮑ Give group members the chance to discuss other parts of this section that they want to comment on or ask questions about.

⮑ Conclude your session, if you wish, by watching this video of The Byrds, in a reunion concert, playing "Turn, Turn, Turn," their song based on the opening poem in this section: www.youtube.com/watch?v=nA2IYnGRYac. If you can't find the video by using this link, search for it online. (Note: David Crosby's weight gain is a side effect of medication to prevent a liver transplant from being rejected. "A time to heal . . .")

THE PRACTICAL RESPONSE TO THESE INSIGHTS

Book of Ecclesiastes > Fifth Major Reflection

INTRODUCTION

A transition now occurs in the extended discourse in Ecclesiastes. To this point, the Teacher has been trying to demonstrate, from experience and observation, that the way most people live "under the sun" is not wise. They wear themselves out, foregoing most of life's present joys, to try to attain results they're hoping for in the future. But there's no guarantee that these results will ever be achieved, and even if they are, they'll disappear and be forgotten in a relatively short time. And so the Teacher has repeatedly counseled a different approach: pursuing projects that we find satisfying and fulfilling while we're doing them (that *might* turn out well in the longer term), and which still leave us the time and energy to enjoy life while we're living it.

Having demonstrated how uncertain life really is—it's both unpredictable and not fully understandable—the Teacher turns to discuss the attitude we should consequently bring to our endeavors. He counsels a restrained, balanced approach, avoiding extremes, cultivating contentment, and being appropriately humble, serious, and cautious, even while seeking to enjoy life in the present.

As the discourse moves into this fifth major reflection (which characteristically culminates in a call for people to "eat and drink and be glad"
and find "joy . . . in their toil"), there's a change in the way the shorter reflections within it are introduced and concluded. Previously such shorter
reflections were introduced by descriptions of what the Teacher "saw . . .
under the sun," and they were concluded with the observation that "this
too is meaningless (*hebel*), a chasing after the wind." The first shorter
reflection in this section is introduced and concluded this way, providing
continuity; but the rest follow a new pattern: They end with a declaration
of the uncertainty of life. They often use the specific term *discover* to describe people's futile efforts to understand life. (The last reflection repeats
this term three times; it's translated "discover" or "comprehend.")

READING

Have different people read the shorter reflections that make up this
section. They begin:

- "I have seen another evil under the sun . . ."
- "Whatever exists has already been named . . ."
- "A good name is better than fine perfume . . ."
- "In this meaningless life of mine I have seen both of these . . ."
- "So I turned my mind to understand . . ."
- "Who is like the wise?" ending, "Even if the wise claim
  they know, they cannot really comprehend (*discover*) it."

DISCUSSION

1 The first two shorter reflections introduce the themes of moderation and contentment that will be developed throughout this fifth
major reflection. They ask, how many children do you need to have—a
hundred? How long do you need to live—a couple thousand years? Every
time you see something you don't have, do you need to try to get it? At
some point people have to stop acquiring and extending so they can start

enjoying what they do have. Otherwise, they may as well have never lived in the first place.

➲ It's been said that just beyond "enough" lies "too much." How much will be "enough" for you? How large a house will you need for yourself and your family? How much of your time and effort will you need to spend making money; when will you honestly have enough to live on? How high a position will you need to fulfill your life's purpose and have a positive influence on the world; what kind of position would be "too high" and interfere with this?

2 The next reflection (beginning "a good name is better than fine perfume") is made up of a series of proverbs that encourage people to accept and embrace the serious side of life and not always be looking for diversions, amusement, and entertainment. These proverbs encourage the qualities of patience, self-control, and contentment, and stress that we must accept that we'll have both good times and bad times.

➲ As a group, watch this Bud Light "Stranded" commercial and discuss what message it sends about what really matters in life: www.youtube.com/watch?v=zE7wyUmsM0k. (If you can't find the commercial using this link, search for it online.) Think about other commercials you've seen for cars, restaurants, electronics, etc. Do they depict the quiet, serious side of life, or do they encourage an escape from it? Choose a product and design a commercial for it that appeals to the qualities of patience, self-control, quietness, and contentment.

➲ What's the difference between the *enjoyment* of life that the Teacher commends and the *amusement* he warns against as a perpetual pursuit?

➲ How prepared are you for bad times when they come, and how accepting of them are you when you're going through them? Are you surprised and offended when God allows you to experience difficulties in life?

3 One of the most controversial statements in the book of Ecclesiastes is found in this section: "I have found one upright man among a thousand, but not one upright woman among them all." But this statement may not reflect the Teacher's own perspective. Instead, it may be a popular saying of the day that he's quoting in order to disagree with it.

A moment earlier in the discourse, he describes a "woman who is a snare, whose heart is a trap and whose hands are chains." He says, "The man who pleases God will escape her." He realizes this may cause his listeners to think he disparages all women. So he clarifies that there are some things he's "not finding" to be true in his reflections on life—including the popular idea that there may be one upright man in a thousand, but never an upright woman. Instead, the Teacher says, "This only have I found": God made *everyone* upright (men and women), but they've all gone astray ("in search of many schemes").

➲ Even if the Teacher doesn't really disparage all women, why does he describe a certain kind of woman by using the images of a snare, a trap, and chains? Do these images apply accurately to some women? Could a man also use these images inappropriately, because he sees the woman in his life as an obstacle to his "chasing after the wind"?

➲ Once again give group members the chance to discuss other parts of this section that they have comments or questions about.

CONCLUDING THOUGHTS AND OBSERVATIONS: "REMEMBER YOUR CREATOR"

Book of Ecclesiastes > Sixth and Seventh Major Reflections
Book of Ecclesiastes > Epilogue

INTRODUCTION

The last part of the book of Ecclesiastes sums up all that has been said previously. The Teacher says literally, "So I reflected *on all this* and concluded *about all this* . . ." The admonition for people to eat and drink and enjoy their work is repeated twice in this section, creating the sixth and seventh major reflections in the book. The sixth is relatively brief, in order to highlight this recurring admonition as the Teacher begins to wind up his discourse. The seventh major reflection is longer, and it's characteristically built out of a series of shorter reflections. These reflections now conclude with a different phrase: the Teacher stresses the unpredictability of life by saying "no one knows" or "you do not know" what is to come.

This seventh and final major reflection is followed by a poem, just as poems came before and after the first major reflection in the book. This poem is a symbolic description of old age, designed to reinforce the advice to "be happy while you are young . . . before the days of trouble come."

The Teacher's discourse ends as it began, with the declaration, "Meaningless! Meaningless! Everything is meaningless!" That is, the future earthly rewards that people hope and strive for are not a reliable source of enduring meaning.

The book concludes with an epilogue written by someone who knew the Teacher, or at least knew about him, and who wants to recommend his sayings to others—with a warning, worthy of the Teacher himself, to use appropriate moderation in studying and following them.

READING

Have someone read the sixth major reflection in the book, beginning "So I reflected on all this" and ending "there is neither working nor planning nor knowledge nor wisdom."

Then have people read the shorter reflections that make up the seventh major reflection. They begin:
- "I have seen something else under the sun . . ."
- "I also saw under the sun . . ."
- "Woe to the land whose king was a servant . . ."
- "If clouds are full of water, they pour rain on the earth."
- "Light is sweet, and it pleases the eyes to see the sun," ending "youth and vigor are meaningless" (fleeting).

Have someone read the poem that follows this major reflection, beginning "Remember your Creator in the days of your youth" and ending "the spirit returns to God who gave it."

Finally, have someone read the closing declaration ("Meaningless! . . . Everything is meaningless!") and the epilogue to the book.

DISCUSSION

1 The sixth major reflection in Ecclesiastes considers the observation that everyone, no matter how they've lived, dies in the end. They're never seen again, and relatively quickly they're forgotten. As we've already noted, the book deliberately limits its perspective to what happens on earth, and this is one of the places where that perspective is felt most keenly. People who believe in an afterlife will be troubled by the Teacher's description of the dead as having no knowledge or emotions and not pursuing any activities. But these statements don't necessarily negate other biblical teachings about heaven and the resurrection. Rather, *from our perspective today on earth*, the dead are simply gone. "Never again will they have a part in anything that happens under the sun." The Teacher's statements are intended to affirm this world as a place of unique joys and passions that a person has the opportunity to experience only once. He wants us to value and appreciate this opportunity and not miss it by pursuing elusive rewards in the future or by disparaging this life in favor of the next.

⮑ What will you miss most about this world when you have to leave it—even if you expect to go to a "better place" when you die? (If you don't think you'll miss anything, explain why.)

⮑ A country/gospel song says, "This world is not my home, I'm just a-passin' through." Do you agree or disagree? Why?

⮑ When the overall conclusion of the book is repeated after this reflection, the Teacher adds something to his recurring advice about eating and drinking and enjoying your work. He says, "Enjoy life with your wife, whom you love." We've already heard him acknowledge that people who invest in relationships in general have a "good return for their labor." What is the payoff in this life of making a marriage, specifically, last?

2 The seventh major reflection in the book is made up mostly of short proverbs. Each one of them is an "example of wisdom." The Teacher begins with proverbs that draw contrasts between the wise and the foolish or provide specific illustrations of wise conduct. The next set of proverbs (beginning "Through laziness, the rafters sag") encourages people to be diligent, discreet, and decisive, and to maintain a "balanced portfolio," pursuing a variety of endeavors because of the uncertainty of life.

⮎ Several of the sayings that illustrate wise conduct show how, in addition to working hard and having the right resources, it's necessary to have skill ("wisdom") in order to succeed. Look at the series of proverbs that begins "whoever digs a pit may fall into it" and ends "the charmer receives no fee." What six activities are being described? What minimum expertise is required for each one?

⮎ In the context of the book as a whole, the implication is that if you do something with greater skill, and thus greater effectiveness, you'll also have greater enjoyment. Describe an activity that you've become skillful enough at to get past the "hard slogging" stage, so that you now get a "rush" from it.

⮎ Other sayings praise the wisdom of making a variety of investments in life, including both short-term and long-term ones. ("After many days you may receive a return"; "Invest in seven ventures, yes, in eight"; "Sow your seed in the morning and at evening let your hands not be idle, for you do not know which will succeed.") Do you have a "balanced portfolio," in terms of how you're investing your finances, time, energy, and hopes? Or do you have "all of your eggs in one basket"? What beliefs about the future, and how much control we have over it, are expressed by these contrasting approaches?

⊃ Another controversial saying is found in this section: "Money is the answer for everything." In context, however, this may simply mean that while "a feast is made for laughter" and "wine makes life merry," money is required for all of this (in the Hebrew idiom, "money *answers* to all [of this]"). The point is that if you're going to enjoy the pleasures of this life, you've got to have at least some money—thus the admonitions to be diligent and manage your resources responsibly. Which of the following best describes the approach you'd like to take to this?

a. If we've met all our obligations and still have some money left over, we can use that for recreation.

b. We set aside a certain amount in our budget for recreation to make sure it happens, no matter what else comes up.

c. We go out and have fun whenever we feel like it, and worry about paying for it later.

3 This reflection culminates in a final repetition of the admonition to enjoy this life while we're living it. Young people are told to "follow the ways of your heart and whatever your eyes see, but know that for all these things God will bring you into judgment." In other words, fulfill your desires and pursue your ambitions wholeheartedly, but be restrained by the knowledge that you'll have to answer to God for everything you do.

⊃ Is this a good enough moral rule in life? Explain.

4 The poem at the end of Ecclesiastes symbolically describes the failing health of old age. Light has been used throughout the book as a symbol for life (those who are alive, for example, are described as those who "see the sun"). Now fading life is depicted by the sun, moon, and stars growing dim and the sky becoming overcast. In the symbolism of this poem, the "keepers of the house" that tremble are the hands; the "strong men" that stoop are the legs. The teeth are the "grinders" that "are few" and "cease," the eyes are "those looking through the windows" who "grow dim," and the ears are the "doors to the street" that close so that the "sound of grinding fades." The almond blossoms probably represent white hair, and the injured grasshopper symbolizes difficulty walking. Some characteristics of old age are described more literally, such as having trouble sleeping and being afraid of heights and robbers. The overall portrait is designed to make people look ahead to the time when their physical capabilities will be much more limited, to get them to use those capabilities in the most meaningful ways possible now, while they still have them.

⮑ Proverbs insists that we should respect the elderly. Is the Teacher doing that here?

⮑ Picture yourself near the end of your life, sitting in a wheelchair with trembling limbs, no teeth, dim eyes, and deaf ears. What does this picture—the one that Ecclesiastes leaves us with—make you want to go out and do while you still can?

⮑ What is your overall response to the ideas expressed in Ecclesiastes? How has this book been helpful to you? How has it perhaps disrupted or conflicted with the way you tend to approach life?

JAMES

EXPERIENCING THE BOOK OF JAMES AS A WHOLE

Book of James (Overview)

INTRODUCTION

Read this introduction aloud in your group and give people a chance to ask questions about it before reading through James together.

Although the book of James has typically been treated as a letter (like Paul's epistles to the Romans or the Ephesians), it's not really a letter at all. Even though it begins like a letter, it doesn't develop like one. Instead, it's a collection of sayings and observations about life, written in the same stream of wisdom teaching that flows through Proverbs and Ecclesiastes.

Like the teachers and sages whose sayings are recorded in those books, James stresses the importance of practical wisdom for living a "good life." In keeping with the message of Proverbs, James identifies the "heart" as the driving force behind what people say and do, and he urges his readers to cultivate character qualities such as perseverance, self-control in speech, justice, and generosity to the poor. And like the Teacher in Ecclesiastes, James warns about the unpredictability of life. Using the Teacher's characteristic language and imagery, he insists, "You *do not even know* what will happen tomorrow. What is your life? You are a *mist* that appears for a little while and then vanishes."

Nevertheless, James transforms the tradition of wisdom teaching as he carries it forward into the new realm of spiritual life that was introduced with the coming of Jesus. There were wisdom teachers in many different countries in the ancient world, and they all drew freely on one another's work. But the teachers in Israel had the unique insight that the "fear of the LORD" was the "beginning of wisdom." That is, a wise and prudent life began by having a proper relationship with the God who created the world and established the conditions of human existence. James envisions this relationship being raised to a higher and more intimate level as it becomes a personal relationship of faith and trust in God through Jesus Christ. And so throughout the book he speaks of "faith," rather than the "fear of the LORD," as the essential quality of a person who's living a life of wisdom.

Like Ecclesiastes, the book of James is a loosely organized discourse that incorporates shorter sayings, such as, "Everyone should be quick to listen, slow to speak and slow to become angry." The discourse in James is built out of short blocks of teaching that begin by addressing readers directly ("my brothers and sisters") or by describing a specific category of people ("believers in humble circumstances," "those who persevere under trial," etc.). Many interpreters believe that these are summaries of, or excerpts from, messages that James gave in the synagogues of Palestine in the years after Jesus' death and resurrection. James was actually the half-brother of Jesus and an important leader in the early community of his followers. James often alludes to sayings of Jesus, to show that he's passing on his teachings.

James uses many of the characteristic devices that synagogue speakers employed at the time, such as addressing listeners directly, asking rhetorical questions (that is, questions whose answers aren't supplied because they're supposed to be obvious), and answering objections raised by imaginary opponents. These teachings were gathered into a collection by James or another member of the community, and sent out like a letter to a wider audience of Jesus' followers throughout the Roman Empire.

(These followers are described symbolically as the "twelve tribes scattered among the nations," meaning God's people all around the world.)

Within the book, the teachings aren't grouped together by topic, so the book doesn't develop logically or systematically. Instead, teachings on various subjects are mixed together, so that each one can strike the reader with fresh impact, like the sayings collected in Proverbs. Nevertheless, a few large themes that are of particular interest and concern to James recur throughout the book and give it an overall unity. These include perseverance in times of trial, justice for the poor, gracious and prudent speech, and how faith in Jesus (like the "fear of the LORD" in Proverbs) leads to "righteous" living. We'll look at these themes in the sessions ahead, after reading through the whole book in this session.

READING

Read through the book of James out loud together. This should take about 15 minutes. (It's on pages 1687–91 in *The Books of The Bible*. If you're using another edition, you can find James in the table of contents.)

Have people take turns reading the individual teachings that make up the book. They're separated by a line of white space in *The Books of The Bible*. (The person who starts should read the letter-like opening and the first teaching after it.) If you're using a different edition, you can recognize the teachings by the way they address readers near their start as "brethren," "brothers," or "brothers and sisters" (depending on your translation), or else describe a particular category of people.

As you listen to the book, note how the teachings flow back and forth among the few key themes mentioned above.

DISCUSSION

⮑ Which of the things that James says struck you the most? Why? (Everyone in the group should try to mention at least one thing.)

⊃ In what ways did the book of James remind you of Proverbs and Ecclesiastes? Where did you see the emphases of the wisdom tradition coming out? How was the experience of reading this book different from the experiences you had with Proverbs and Ecclesiastes?

⊃ If you attend the worship gatherings of a community of Jesus' followers, then based on these excerpts and summaries of James's teaching, would you like him to be one of the regular speakers there? Why or why not?

THE VALUE OF TRIALS

INTRODUCTION

The teachings of James that were sent throughout the Roman Empire arose from his experience as a leader of the community of Jesus' followers in Palestine. From these teachings we get a glimpse into the challenges that community was facing in the first decades after Jesus' death and resurrection.

For one thing, James says that his audience is "suffering," that they're facing "trials of many kinds." This probably refers to the way the people James customarily spoke to, who were primarily Jewish and still attending the synagogues, were persecuted by their leaders and neighbors because of their faith in Jesus. He tells his listeners they should rejoice in these trials, because they'll make them more patient and persevering if they stand firm. James encourages suffering believers to turn to God in prayer for strength and deliverance, and to ask for wisdom to know how to navigate through these difficult times.

The trials James refers to may also include the poverty that most of his listeners lived in, as well as disputes that flared between individuals and groups within the community. We'll look more at those two things in later sessions. In this session, we'll explore the value that James finds in trials of all kinds as occasions for drawing closer to God and developing mature character.

READING AND DISCUSSION

1 Have someone read the opening teaching in the book of James, beginning "Consider it pure joy, my brothers and sisters, whenever you face trials" and ending, "they are double-minded and unstable in all they do."

This first teaching in the book speaks directly to the trials that many believers were experiencing. James says difficulties like these are an occasion for us to develop an important character quality: *perseverance*. The term he uses means literally staying in place and standing your ground, rather than running away. He praises the same quality in another teaching shortly afterwards: "Blessed are those who *persevere* under trial, because when they have stood the test, they will receive the crown of life that God has promised to those who love him."

James says that suffering can also develop *patience* in us. This term refers to a person's ability to keep things under control on the inside, so that they can endure tough situations. James uses this term three times as he encourages his listeners to await Jesus' return and the deliverance it will bring: "Be *patient*, then, brothers and sisters, until the Lord's coming. See how the farmer waits for the land to yield its valuable crop, *patiently waiting* for the autumn and spring rains. You too, be *patient* and stand firm, because the Lord's coming is near." Right afterwards James uses both terms together: "Brothers and sisters, as an example of *patience* in the face of suffering, take the prophets who spoke in the name of the Lord. As you know, we count as blessed those who have *persevered*."

⮑ Have you ever had an experience where you "stayed in place" in a difficult situation, even though you felt like running away, because you believed God wanted you there? What did you learn, and how did you grow, because you stayed put? Did something good come out of the situation in the end?

➲ Think of the greatest difficulty you're facing in life right now. How well do you have things under control on the inside as you deal with it?

a. By God's grace, I'm holding it together pretty well.

b. Some days I keep it together and other days I fall apart.

c. I'm totally freaking out inside and just about ready to bail!

Pray for one another, that in these difficulties God will help you develop greater patience so you can hold things together well on the inside and see the situations through.

2 In the opening teaching of the book, James also describes trials as an occasion to draw close to God in prayer (specifically, to ask for the wisdom needed to face the trial). At the end of the book, he describes a wider variety of circumstances that are also occasions for prayer. Once again he encourages those who are in trouble (literally "suffering") to pray, but he also urges those in good circumstances to sing praises, and those who are sick to ask for prayer for healing.

- Have someone read the teaching about prayer at the end of the book, beginning "Is anyone among you in trouble?" and ending ". . . the earth produced its crops."

James speaks in this teaching of "the prayer offered *in faith*" and "the prayer of a *righteous* person." (As we'll see in session 25, for James being "righteous" means having faith that translates into just and godly living.) He said similarly in the opening teaching, "when you ask, you must believe" (literally, "ask *in faith*"). When he speaks of praying in "faith," James doesn't mean that if we just believe hard enough, we can make something happen. Instead, faith means having an unwavering personal trust and confidence in God. It's the opposite of doubt, which means being divided in our intentions: "Well, maybe I'll trust God with this, and maybe I won't; I'm working on a 'plan B' in case I decide God isn't going to come through for me."

➲ What reasons can you give why you should have confidence in God to help you in your present situation? Are there reasons why you might have difficulty trusting God? Share these reasons with the group if you're comfortable, and see if someone can help address your concerns.

3 James recognizes that going through trials requires a great deal of wisdom, and so in the opening teaching of the book he encourages his listeners to ask God to give them the wisdom they need: "If any of you lacks wisdom, you should ask God, who gives generously to all without finding fault, and it will be given to you." Shortly afterwards he expands on this idea of God being the giver of all good gifts: "Don't be deceived, my dear brothers and sisters. Every good and perfect gift is from above, coming down from the Father of the heavenly lights, who does not change like shifting shadows." A later teaching in the book speaks of wisdom specifically as one of the good gifts that comes down to us out of heaven from God.

- Have someone read the teaching in the middle of the book that begins "Who is wise and understanding among you?" and ends "Peacemakers who sow in peace reap a harvest of righteousness."

➲ Do you see God as someone who loves to give good gifts to people? What helps you see God this way, or hinders you?

➲ James describes the "wisdom that comes from heaven" as "first of all pure; then peace-loving, considerate, submissive, full of mercy and good fruit, impartial and sincere." Which of these characteristics would you most like to have more of?

➲ The Greeks thought of "wisdom" as the quality of a mind that was well-educated and adept at speculative reasoning. Jews living in the Roman Empire were influenced by this understanding. But this kind of "wisdom," James points out, frequently leads to arguments and disputes. And so he encourages his listeners to cultivate instead the kind of "wisdom" that was praised in their own tradition: devotion to God that produces exemplary character qualities. How is "wisdom" (or the equivalent) defined in your own culture? If you can, quote a saying that expresses this definition succinctly. How would you critique your culture's definition of wisdom from a biblical perspective?

⮑ James describes wisdom as the free gift of a generous God (just as Ecclesiastes says that the ability to enjoy life and find satisfaction in one's work is a "gift from God"). But Proverbs depicts wisdom as something that's developed slowly in a heart that's being reshaped by teaching and experience. Are these ideas compatible? Have you ever experienced wisdom (the knowledge of how to conduct yourself in life) as something God gave you for the asking? Is it fair to get wisdom this way, rather than through the "school of hard knocks"?

THE RICH AND THE POOR
FROM GOD'S PERSPECTIVE

INTRODUCTION

As we noted in the previous session, the people James customarily spoke to were mostly poor. Palestine in his day was largely agricultural; land and wealth were concentrated in the hands of a few. Most of the population worked as tenant farmers or day laborers. The rich were using their advantages in power and wealth to force the few remaining small landholders off their property. James describes the rich "exploiting" the poor and "dragging [them] into court" to seize their lands. The wealthy class was hostile to those who believed in Jesus because his teachings were considered a destabilizing threat to the existing order. That's why James also says to his listeners that the rich are "blaspheming the noble name of him to whom you belong." The book addresses both rich and poor to show them how they should view their present circumstances and how they should relate to one another.

READING AND DISCUSSION

1 After beginning his book by addressing the trials his community was undergoing, James speaks in the very next teaching about the other defining reality of their experience: their poverty. He says, paradoxically, that "believers in humble circumstances ought to take pride in their high position. But the rich should take pride in their humiliation." He means that if someone is a believer, even if they are poor, they should recognize that they are ultimately very honored because God has chosen them to belong to his people. And if someone is rich, they should adopt a humble attitude to acknowledge that their advantages of wealth and status are only temporary ("fleeting," the Teacher would say) and that God will ultimately eliminate all such distinctions between people. The rich "will pass away like a wild flower. For the sun rises with scorching heat and withers the plant; its blossom falls and its beauty is destroyed. In the same way, the rich will fade away even while they go about their business."

⤵ Do you see yourself as rich or poor? If you're poor, do you nevertheless see yourself as honored because you belong to God? If you're rich, are you humbled by the knowledge that your riches will soon pass away?

2 While he encourages his listeners to put their present circumstances in perspective by remembering that God will ultimately set things right on earth, James isn't content to put up with inequality until then. In a later teaching he attacks the way the rich were treated with favoritism in the synagogues, where believers in Jesus continued to worship in his day.

- Have someone read the teaching a little later in the book of James that begins "My brothers and sisters, believers in our glorious Lord Jesus Christ must not show favoritism" and ends ". . . you have become a lawbreaker."

⤵ Why do you think the poor in these synagogues were treating the rich with favoritism, even though the rich were exploiting and oppressing them?

➲ James says that God has "chosen those who are poor in the eyes of the world to be rich in faith and to inherit the kingdom." As a general rule, the poorer a person is, the more open they are to hearing and believing the good news about Jesus. Why do you think this is so?

➲ Honestly, how would a "poor person in filthy old clothes" be treated if they came to your church?

➲ In what ways are the rich treated with favoritism within communities of Jesus' followers today? What would it look like for us to follow James's teaching about not showing favoritism?

3 Have someone read the teaching towards the end of the book of James that begins "Now listen, you rich people, weep and wail because of the misery that is coming on you" and ends, "You have condemned and murdered the innocent one, who was not opposing you."

James ultimately addresses the rich directly and warns them, in very harsh terms, that divine judgment is coming upon them because they've cheated their workers and killed those who tried to get justice. As they've lived in "luxury and self-indulgence," they've really just "fattened" themselves up for the "day of slaughter." James alludes to a saying of Jesus, "Do not store up for yourselves treasures on earth, where moth and rust destroy," to put his authority behind this warning. James says to the rich, "Moths have eaten your clothes. Your gold and silver are corroded" (literally "rusted"); "you have hoarded wealth" (literally "stored up treasure") "in the last days."

➲ If a person is living in "luxury and self-indulgence" and "fattening themselves up," is this inevitably happening at someone else's expense? In other words, if one person or group or country has far more than enough, does this mean others must have less than they need? Follow up on the discussion you had in session 13 about how people can use their buying power and consumer choices to help, rather than hurt, those living in poverty. Have you begun to do this in some new practical ways? If so, tell your group about it.

⮑ Are great inequalities in wealth always created through injustice? Explain.

⮑ What people and organizations do you know about that are working effectively to overcome poverty and inequity by upholding justice? As a group, pray for these people and organizations and their work.

⮑ Do you think James is announcing that judgment is inevitable against these exploitative and oppressive rich people? Or is he trying to get them to change by warning them what consequences they're facing? In other words, is it too late for them, or do they still have a chance?

KEEPING A TIGHT REIN ON THE TONGUE

INTRODUCTION

Perhaps because of the pressures of persecution and poverty, and perhaps also because of human nature, people in the communities that James spoke to were having angry "fights and quarrels." These conflicts were aggravated by the harsh and unkind things that people were saying: They were slandering one another and not keeping "a tight reign on their tongues." James saw that the quarrels fueled by these unrestrained words were undermining the essential purpose of the community of Jesus' followers: "Those who consider themselves religious and yet do not keep a tight rein on their tongues deceive themselves, and their religion is worthless. Religion that God our Father accepts as pure and faultless is this: to look after orphans and widows in their distress and to keep oneself from being polluted by the world." And so James uses the occasion of these conflicts to reassert the wisdom tradition's teaching about the importance of self-control in speech.

READING AND DISCUSSION

1 Have someone read the teaching in the middle of the book of James that begins, "Not many of you should presume to be teachers, my brothers and sisters," and ends, "Neither can a salt spring produce fresh water."

In this teaching James uses examples from the natural world to illustrate a number of observations about human speech. He notes, first of all, by analogy to horses' bridles and ships' rudders, that something small can direct something large and powerful. The tongue, he says, is only a "small part of the body," but it can determine the "whole course of one's life." When it's used in destructive ways, the results can be devastating: "Consider what a great forest is set on fire by a small spark."

James then observes that while every kind of wild animal can be tamed, "no one can tame the tongue." Finally, he observes how unnatural it is for "praise and cursing" to come "out of the same mouth." A spring doesn't send both fresh and salty water out of the same opening. Grape vines and fig trees only produce one kind of fruit. (This is likely an allusion to another one of Jesus' sayings: "Do people pick grapes from thornbushes, or figs from thistles?") So why should the same mouth praise God but curse people who are made in the image of God? "My brothers and sisters," James protests, "this should not be."

⮩ James warns that our words can determine our "whole course of life." What examples can you give of people whose lives have taken a major turn, for better or for worse, because of something they said?

⮩ James suggests here that if we speak badly about other people, we're contradicting any praises we may offer to God. He says in an earlier teaching that if we don't control our speech, our religion is "worthless." And here he describes the unrestrained tongue as "set on fire by hell." The suggestion is that spiritual victory or defeat in our lives and communities depends greatly on how we speak to one another. What can you say to someone in the coming week that will help win a spiritual victory or reverse a spiritual defeat?

⊃ The wisdom tradition emphasizes self-control in speech. Proverbs says, "Those who have knowledge use words with restraint." The Teacher warns in Ecclesiastes, "Do not be quick with your mouth, do not be hasty in your heart to utter anything before God. God is in heaven and you are on earth, so let your words be few." Elsewhere in this book, James encourages his listeners to "keep a tight rein on their tongues." But here he says that "no one can tame the tongue." He adds that it's a "restless evil, full of deadly poison." What point do you think he's trying to make by saying things like this, if he really does want people to try to tame their tongues?

2 James's teachings about speech extend beyond his warnings about the destructive effects of harsh words between people. He also cautions his listeners against boasting. Many had been bragging about the profits they expected to make in business. While Palestine, as we've noted, was largely agricultural at this time, there was increasing trading activity as the rich tried to make profitable investments in commodities and the poor tried to escape poverty by entering the merchant class.

- Have someone read the teaching near the end of the book that begins, "Now listen, you who say, 'Today or tomorrow we will go to this or that city . . .'" and ends, "if you know the good you ought to do and don't do it, you sin."

⊃ James says that it's "sin" and "evil" to make boasts based on what we presume we'll accomplish in the future, when our lives are so uncertain. Divide your group into twos or threes and have people practice with each other how to describe their future hopes, plans, and ambitions in ways that acknowledge that God rules over the whole world and that their own lives are fragile and uncertain.

3 At several more places in the book James warns against other kinds of harmful speech. Form three teams and have each one create and perform a brief skit that illustrates one of the following teachings and includes God as one of the characters:

➲ "Don't grumble against one another, brothers and sisters, or you will be judged. The Judge is standing at the door!"

➲ "Above all, my brothers and sisters, do not swear—not by heaven or by earth or by anything else. All you need to say is a simple 'Yes' or 'No.' Otherwise you will be condemned."

➲ "My dear brothers and sisters, take note of this: Everyone should be quick to listen, slow to speak and slow to become angry, because our anger does not produce the righteousness that God desires."

➲ "Brothers and sisters, do not slander one another. Anyone who speaks against a brother or sister or judges them speaks against the law and judges it. When you judge the law, you are not keeping it, but sitting in judgment on it. There is only one Lawgiver and Judge, the one who is able to save and destroy. But you—who are you to judge your neighbor?"

THE LIFE THAT FLOWS FROM A NEW HEART

INTRODUCTION

The teaching in the book of James, like the wise counsel in the books of Proverbs and Ecclesiastes, is meant for a specific kind of person. James intends his advice about how to handle trials, poverty, and conflicts for people who are in a liberating and empowering relationship with God. At various points in the book he talks directly about how to enter into and sustain this relationship.

READING AND DISCUSSION

1 For James, as we've already seen, "faith" plays the role that the "fear of the LORD" does in Proverbs. It's the inner dynamic that flows out into a life that's "righteous," meaning well-lived, in accordance with God's ways. But James needs to correct some wrong ideas about what "faith" really is. These ideas may have come from a misunderstanding of what the apostle Paul (whose teachings were already circulating at this time) meant when he said that people are saved "through faith" and "not by works." Some of James's listeners were apparently taking this to mean that having the right beliefs was all that really mattered. James, in keeping with the characteristic emphasis of the wisdom tradition, counters that what really matters is how our faith translates into practical living. If our living is wrong, then our faith must be deficient.

- Have someone read the teaching near the middle of the book that begins, "What good is it, my brothers and sisters, if people claim to have faith but have no deeds?" and ends, "As the body without the spirit is dead, so faith without deeds is dead."

The issue here is what determines that a person has been "saved." In the Bible, "salvation" or "being saved" is a rich concept that includes being brought back into relationship with God, forgiven for what we've done wrong, restored to a life of meaning and purpose, and delivered from the control of a world system that's opposed to God.

When James says we need to have "deeds" (or "works") to be saved, he doesn't mean that we have to make ourselves good enough for God. We don't have to put the pieces of our own lives together. James describes salvation as something we receive freely from God: It's one of the "good and perfect" gifts that comes down "from the Father."

But James does insist that if a person is genuinely saved, righteous "deeds" will follow. So-called "faith" that makes no difference in a person's life is really no faith at all—it's "dead."

⮑ Have you received salvation as a "good and perfect gift" from God? If you don't think you have, find someone in the group who believes they have and interview them in front of the others to ask when and how this happened. (The group can do a number of interviews if it would like.)

⮑ Drawing on what James says here and on your own reflections, describe what kinds of "deeds" give credible evidence that a person's faith is truly alive.

2 Have someone read the teaching near the beginning of the book that begins, "Do not merely listen to the word, and so deceive yourselves," and ends, "they will be blessed in what they do."

Besides "faith" and "deeds," James uses some further terms to talk about salvation. He says in his other teachings, as we've seen, that God "chose to give us birth through the word of truth," and that to receive salvation we need to "humbly accept the word planted in you, which can save you." In this teaching he says that this "word" is equivalent to a "law that gives freedom." (James says elsewhere that we should "speak and act as those who are going to be judged by the law that gives freedom.") His listeners were primarily Jewish, and they understood their law, with all of its commandments, to be God's word to them through Moses. But James expands the meaning of God's word and law beyond this traditional understanding.

In the early communities of Jesus' followers, the "word of truth" was another term for the gospel, meaning the good news about Jesus as Savior. Jesus himself was also called the "Word." So being born of God "through the word of truth" and "humbly accept[ing] the word" means experiencing new life by believing the good news about Jesus.

Elsewhere in the book, in his warning against favoritism, James calls the commandment to "love your neighbor as yourself" a "royal law" (or "king's law"). This is another allusion to a saying of Jesus, who taught that all of the requirements in the Law of Moses could be summed by the commandments to love God with all your heart and to love your neighbor as yourself. According to James, this is the "king's law," or governing authority, in the community of Jesus' followers. This law "gives freedom" by simply stating the goal that must govern our actions—expressing love for others—and leaving the specifics up to us. The people of God are no longer identified by how they follow the Law of Moses, but by how they show genuine love for others as they creatively live out the new life God has put in them.

⊃ Do you like the idea of a "law that gives freedom," which specifies that love for others must be the goal of all your actions and then leaves the specifics up to you?

3 Have someone read the teaching near the middle of the book that begins, "What causes fights and quarrels among you?" and ends, "Humble yourselves before the Lord, and he will lift you up."

As James addresses the "fights and quarrels" in his communities, he identifies the spiritual problem behind them, and in the process he describes salvation in one more way. He explains to his listeners that they're fighting because they're being driven by their "desires." (He says similarly at the start of the book, "Each of you is tempted when you are dragged away by your own evil desire and enticed.") In other words, they're going after the things of "the world" (possessions, advancement, pleasures—all the things the Teacher showed were temporary, precarious, and uncertain) as if they provided the deepest meaning in life. This has set them on a course against God. They need to "humble [them]selves before the Lord," ask forgiveness, and resist temptation. At the center of James's correction here is the admonition to *purify your hearts*. This brings us back to where we began in the book of Proverbs: everyone has a "heart," a core-of-being, and everything they do flows from it. For people to turn from the callous, greedy, violent life James is describing here and become capable of the kind of "deeds" that demonstrate genuine "faith," their hearts need to be transformed through the influence of the Spirit that God "has caused to dwell in us." In other words, being saved means getting a new heart.

⊃ Conclude your study of the book of James by praying together based on this last teaching you've just read. People can pray either silently or out loud. In their prayers, people can express sorrow for doing wrong and humility in returning to God; they can ask for help in resisting temptation; they can thank God for giving his Spirit to live inside us. As a group, pray together with anyone who wants to ask God for a new heart.

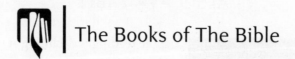 The Books of The Bible

Clean. Beautiful. Unshackled.

- chapter and verse numbers removed
  (chapter and verse range given at bottom of page)
- natural literary breaks
- no additives: notes, cross-references,
  and section headings removed
- single-column setting
- whole books restored (Luke-Acts)
- book order provides greater help in understanding

There is no Bible more suited to reading—from the beginning of the book to the end—than *The Books of The Bible*. This "new" approach is actually the original approach, and I love it.

Scot McKnight
North Park University

For more information or to download the gospel of John, visit http://www.thebooksofthebible.info. Premium editions of this Bible will be available in Spring 2011 from Zondervan at your favorite Christian retailer.

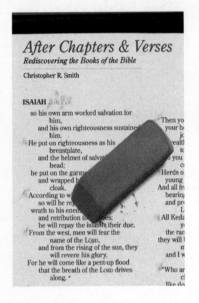

Bible reading is declining at such a rapid rate that within 30 years the Bible will be a "thing of the past" for most Christ-followers. One of the main reasons for this decline is the format of the Bible. The format we know today was created so that a "modern" world could divide and analyze and systematize the Scriptures. But this made the word of God practically unreadable. As we move into a postmodern world, we'll need to recapture the stories, songs, poems, letters, and dreams that naturally fill the pages of Scripture. Only then will a new generation of readers return to the Bible.

Christopher Smith argues in this book that the "time for chapters and verses is over." He explains how these divisions of the biblical text interfere with our reading and keep us from understanding the Scriptures. He describes how Biblica has created a new format for the Bible, without chapters and verses, with the biblical books presented in their natural forms. And he shares the exciting new approaches people are already taking to reading, studying, preaching, and teaching the Bible in this new presentation.

Paperback, 234 pages, 5.5 x 8.5
ISBN: 978-1-60657-044-9
Retail: $15.99

Available for purchase online or through your local bookstore.